Filled with honesty, humour and wisdom

become a treasure for any parent navigating ... journey of faith with their
children. Buy this book! You'll be glad you did.

Mark and Lindsay Melluish, Directors of New Wine and Pastors of St
Paul's Ealing

*Compassion and hope are the hallmarks of this remarkable book. It is full
of insight and inspiration for any family who has experienced the sadness
of someone dearly loved who takes a different path in life and faith – which
means this book is for everyone! Katharine and Jo help us to see there is
always more to learn as well as infinite possibilities for God's grace to
surprise and abound.*

Rt Revd Paul Williams, Bishop of Kensington

*Given that the subject matter of this book is of such significance for so many,
it is extraordinary it has not been written before. Tackling this sensitive and
emotive issue with great compassion, deep wisdom and disarming honesty,
Keeping Faith will soon be regarded as essential reading for those at any stage
of Christian parenting.*

Revd Paul Langham, author and Vicar of Christ Church Clifton

This book acknowledges the deep pain and disappointment felt by parents whose children decide that the Christian faith is not for them. The book unveils the difficulties children face, challenges some wrong thinking and brings a wonderful message of comfort, grace and hope.

Mark Molden, Chief Executive, Care for the Family

I welcome this brave book that confronts a heart-searing issue for so many parents. I pray many will have the courage to avail themselves of its wisdom and experience – a book the church really needs.

Rico Tice, All Souls Church & Christianity Explored

It is vital that we collectively maintain the momentum in supporting parents and churches in the nurture of their children. This thoughtful and sensitive book does just that, building on the explosive GYKTC initiative that has been so powerful in its impact. I pray that together we will continue to make children and young people our urgent priority.

Tim Hastie-Smith, National Director, Scripture Union

Keeping faith...

Being family when belief is in question

Jo Swinney
Katharine Hill

Printed in India by Nutech Print Services India.
Cover design and internal layout by Heather Knight.

Scripture Union is an international Christian charity working with
churches in more than 130 countries.

Thank you for purchasing this resource. Any profits from this book support
SU in England and Wales to bring the good news of Jesus Christ to children,
young people and families and to enable them to meet God through the Bible
and prayer.

Find out more about our work and how you can get involved at:
www.scriptureunion.org.uk (England and Wales)
www.suscotland.org.uk (Scotland)
www.suni.co.uk (Northern Ireland)
www.scriptureunion.org (USA)
www.su.org.au (Australia)

For George, Charlotte, Ed and Henry Hill and for Alexa and Charis
Swinney … with no strings attached!

Acknowledgements

We would like to thank all those who have helped us make this book possible. We are grateful to Mark Molden, June Way, Sheron Rice, Esther Holt and the great team at Care for the Family for their vision, support and practical help. We want to thank Rob Parsons for his help and encouragement and for writing the foreword, and Miranda Harris (Jo's Mum) for her help with the first draft. 'Tricia Williams, Angela Grigson and the team at Scripture Union have also been wonderful. Our special thanks go to all the parents and young people who have so honestly shared their stories with us, which have brought the book to life. We have changed their names to protect their privacy. And finally, we want to acknowledge our wonderful husbands Richard and Shawn for their constant love, support and encouragement both in writing this book and in the ongoing adventure and privilege of parenting.

Jo Swinney is a writer and speaker, and the editor of *Closer to God*. She also writes regularly for various Christian periodicals and blogs at www.joswinney.com. She lives with a reverend, two funny little girls and a black and white cat in South Bucks. This is her fourth book.

Katharine Hill is Director of Family Policy at Care for the Family and formerly a solicitor specialising in family law. She is an established speaker and writer on marriage and parenting issues. Katharine and her husband Richard have four young adult children and co-authored *Rules of Engagement*, a book for newly engaged couples.

Contents

Foreword

Psychiatrist John White said, 'There is no pain like parental pain.' I would add this: 'There is no *guilt* like parental guilt.' I have spoken with thousands of parents about their prodigal children. More often than not they will say to me, 'I don't know where we went wrong.' I ask, 'What makes you think you went wrong anywhere?' And time and time again they quote from the book of Proverbs, 'Start children off on the way they should go, and even when they are old they will not turn from it' (22:6).

What happens next rarely varies. I say, 'That verse is not a guarantee – it's a general principle. Much of the Bible is about God, the perfect father, saying to his children, "Why have you rebelled against me?"' I then say, 'I know you haven't been perfect parents – none of us has – but what is almost certainly not true is that the total responsibility for your child's lifestyle rests on your shoulders. As our children grow older they will make their own choices – and sometimes those are bad choices.' At that point they often say something like this: 'Nobody ever told us that. The other parents in our church seem to have kids who are wonderful Christians; we often feel total failures. You have no idea what a release it is to realise that even God has trouble with his children.'

Katharine Hill and Jo Swinney have written this wonderful book for parents who feel just like that. I am thrilled because I believe it will be a valuable addition to the resources available through Care for the Family's initiative 'Getting Your Kids Through Church Without Them Ending Up Hating God'. This initiative has now been under way for two years and looks at how the church and we, as parents, can seek to avoid many of the things that can harm our children's faith.

I know that many of you have prayed long and hard for your children for years and, right now, they may seem further away than ever. Other parents will be only just coming to the realisation that their children have chosen not to share their faith. But whatever your circumstances are, this book will be a blessing. Richly honest and open, it addresses difficult, often painful, issues with warmth, practicality, understanding and, above all, hope. I urge you to read it – it's too important to miss.

Rob Parsons OBE

Chairman and Founder, Care for the Family

Chapter 1

Wish you were here

Jo Swinney

When people don't make the same faith choices as their parents it is a big deal; the repercussions can be severe.

In some religions it can put a person's life at risk, or mean that they are no longer welcome in their homes. Christian parents will rarely disinherit their child on the basis of their church attendance, but it can still be a huge issue to work through. The questions are almost too hard to voice: Is it my fault? Has God reneged on his promises to me and to my family? Will my child ever know Jesus, and what about their eternal destiny? Are my Christian friends judging me? Is God? How are we going to stay close to each other when we now have so little in common? Is it wrong that I feel closer to my believing child? Is she ever going to come back to God, and will she have done any lasting damage to herself and to us in the meantime? We can't really overstate how traumatic it can be to watch our child deliberately choose to walk off in a direction we have told him, every way we know how, leads to disaster.

Everybody hurts

But the pain is not just felt by parents. The wider family feels it deeply too – siblings, grandparents, aunts and uncles, cousins – everyone is impacted.

Antonia describes how complicated it has been since her sister Georgie turned her back on Christianity: 'She sees me as an ally, and says "at least you don't care what I believe". The sad thing is that I do, although I would never tell her that. She likes to talk about Mum and Dad with me, how they've damaged her and how ridiculous and narrow-minded she finds them. The problem is I can see their side too. I feel pulled between them.' Antonia is desperate to stay close to her sister, so feels she can't even hint at her own sadness.

Church leaders and particularly children's workers and youth leaders invest hugely in the lives of young people. They also feel a sense of responsibility and failure, just as parents do, when someone decides to go their own way. My husband has been in youth work for over a decade, and nothing discourages him more than reports of people he has mentored and discipled for years throwing it all away in the first term at university. It breaks his heart, especially when they have made a genuine connection with God as teenagers.

So pain is felt by believing siblings, grandparents, church communities – but it is also felt by those at the centre of the drama, the ones who've provoked all this upset. There are multiple reasons why people are not Christians, but you would be pressed to find someone who wasn't one simply because they wanted to hurt their parents, or as a perverse extension of teenage rebellion. Over and over again people convey the pain involved in realising their journey has brought them to an entirely different country from the one in which they grew up. It can be an anguishing process, one in which their sense of identity, belonging and purpose is profoundly shaken. No one wants to have to face the possibility that their parents have made fools of themselves by basing their lives on a myth, or that everything they believed and experienced as a child needs to be reassessed. Belief in eternal life, a loving and involved God, forgiveness and mercy, a purpose and a shared outlook with their parents – all this would in many ways make life easier. But integrity demands that they are true to their own convictions.

It has been a bumpy road for Lizzie. Even now, in her late twenties, I sense her longing that things could have been different. Here are some extracts of the long exchange we had over Facebook:

'Being brought up as a Christian from birth, there was never a time I didn't believe in Christianity. We had nightly quiet times, church every week (including family church when we were on holiday – no escape there!), Bible camp holidays and so on.'

'When I started university I was challenged to question my beliefs, and I discovered I had no reasons of my own for believing. My parents are pretty devout, and they just expected my brother Dave and me to believe and follow too. Leaving Christianity was not a decision – it was something that happened *to* me. I had what Christians call 'doubts' when I was a Christian, but I had never really considered the possibility that my beliefs could actually be *wrong*. Once this ball got rolling, belief became impossible.'

Leaving Christianity was not a decision – it was something that happened to me

'It was an extremely emotional and often painful experience. It probably took about two years before I settled into a new way of thinking. In the intervening period I felt pretty confused and I regularly asked God to give me some evidence that he existed. It all came to a head when I went on a Christian Union weekend away at the end of my second year of university, in the active hope of experiencing God. I didn't experience anything. When I went home for Christmas I talked to Dave about my loss of faith, and it seems to me he lost his faith overnight as a result. He is more forthright than me, so initiated by him we told our parents. I hadn't had the guts to talk to them about it.'

'I'm very aware of how my parents felt about all this, and I've been at pains to explain to them that it was an intellectual realisation and not even something I was in control of. It has been very hard for them to accept, and at first they thought it was just a phase. When they realised it wasn't, they seemed a bit desperate. I think they took it personally at the time and, even now, on the odd occasion we've ended up talking about beliefs, they've referred to me as rejecting God. In some senses, I feel I have lost my

I feel I have lost my parents along with losing my faith

parents along with losing my faith; because their beliefs are so much a part of their lives, we now find it hard to relate to each other.'

We are hardwired to crave our parents' approval and attention: no one likes feeling they are a disappointment or a cause of sorrow or anxiety to those they love. We need to remember this when the matter of faith comes up between us, and bear in mind the pain our children are going through as well as our own. The search for truth and meaning can be frustrating and difficult, and we must be willing to respect people on a genuine quest for answers.

Great expectations

During King Zedekiah's reign, the Lord spoke to a priest called Jeremiah and he said, 'Before I formed you in the womb I knew you, before you were born I set you apart; I appointed you as a prophet to the nations' (Jeremiah 1:5). A great many years passed, and then during the reign of Queen Elizabeth II a woman in the city of Birmingham, West Midlands, fell pregnant. I met her husband when he spoke at my university Christian Union about how this same prophecy also referred to his son. Jeremiah Junior grew up in the knowledge that he was to be a prophet to the nation of China. He was taught Cantonese along with his mother tongue to prepare him for his preordained calling, and one can only imagine that the school playground was a cruel place for him. I have always remembered him, and wondered what it would be like to live under such a crush of parentally-mediated divine expectation.

This is an extreme example, but all parents have hopes and dreams for their children, and it is certainly not a bad thing that they do. What parent would not aspire and work for a good future for their family? These aspirations may be as simple as a vaguely-articulated desire that they be happy and healthy. They may involve more specific ideas around achievement, perhaps that they excel in sport or music. Andre Agassi remembers his father taping a tennis racquet to his forearm when he was only 2 years' old. Some parents covet certain professions for their offspring, or plan to pass on the family firm. The Poulen family, who I just found on Google, have been funeral directors for four generations; the destiny of the fifth seems written in the stars.

Christian parents think of their child as a gift from God, and over and above all other desires we might have for them is the longing that they will know and love Jesus as we do. It frightens me how much I want this for my little girls. I want it because I believe it is true with all my heart. I want it because I think that if they grow into their own knowledge and understanding of God they will live fuller, deeper, richer lives. I want it because I want them to flourish, to have the kinds of characters that the Spirit creates in those he dwells within. In this era and in western cultures, we have been taught to hide our certainties, to be suspicious of our own strongly held convictions. We ought not to be ashamed that we want our children to meet and fall for Jesus as we have. Why on earth would we not want that?

All small children start out seeing the world from the same perspective as their primary carers. Holly's memories will resonate with many: 'I had a great home environment growing up – I have nothing to complain about. My mum

I never questioned Christianity as a child. It was all I knew

and dad are both Christians, but they weren't strict. We all went to church every week, and we said grace at meals and prayed at bedtime. I never questioned Christianity as a child. It was all I knew.'

In the same way, until he was 10 Sean believed that there was no God – unquestioningly accepting his parents' beliefs. He first went to a church when his family was invited to a wedding. He thought the order of service was a menu and tried to order lasagne from an usher. His parents never felt the need to provide him with an array of alternative beliefs when he was small, and if they had it would only have confused him.

Eventually, though, we all begin to question the infallibility of our parents' wisdom. Some wind up coming to the same conclusions, but others don't. There are apples that fall so far from the tree that you can only assume they sprouted wings and migrated to another orchard altogether. Katy Perry of 'I kissed a girl' fame was raised on a restricted diet of church and Bible; the Satanist singer Marilyn Manson's mother is Episcopalian and his father is Catholic; Britney Spears is the daughter of Baptists; Professor Steve Jones,

Secularist of the Year in 2006, spent his boyhood Sundays in church. The Economic and Social Research Council reported findings in August 2005 that half of children with two religious parents reject church as adults. Statistics around religion and belief are notoriously unreliable, as a person's faith is not fixed or innate and cannot be empirically measured, but this hints at how common a situation it is.

Now what?

There's a reason that politics and religion are avoided at parties by those with good manners – even a light-hearted remark is liable to turn up the heat to an unpleasant temperature. People have been martyred over doctrinal nuances, and even with the relative thickness of blood taken into account, families can find a religious divide a real strain. Some take their cue from dinner-party etiquette and do their best to bury the subject. Erica says, 'My second son is quite verbally aggressive about how he was "forced to go to church". He blames his upbringing for his anti-God stance, and we now avoid the subject of faith or church.'

I couldn't bear to disappoint my parents

There are also a lot of people out there faking faith to keep their parents happy, feeling it too traumatic to deal with head-on. Holly continued to go to church for three years after she stopped having any sort of faith of her own, because in her words, 'I couldn't bear to disappoint my parents. Still to this day we haven't had a conversation about it, and they've never asked straight out whether I'm a Christian.'

What we may not factor into a strategy of conflict avoidance for the sake of family peacekeeping is the cost, namely, an authentic relationship with a loved one, in full awareness of who they are and what they think and feel. Our spirituality, whatever its shape and flavour, is deeply entwined with our identity, and by trying to relate to our children without acknowledging that aspect of their personhood we may well have a wizened version of the relationship we could have. Kate is happy about the place she has got to with her son. She says, 'James and I don't see eye to eye on matters of faith at the moment, but we have worked hard to make sure we still connect at a deep level, which means I don't hide my love of Jesus from him, and I think he feels he is free to be himself around me too.'

Other families find that they can't go near a discussion about the spiritual realm without a bust up. Steve says, 'When I started drifting, I kept a low profile, because I didn't want the confrontation. When the topic came up, maybe around Christmas or another event that touched on God, I would be direct about my views. It would end up with Mum crying and Dad being upset. They were very defensive.' Because it is natural to respond from the gut when something we consider precious is criticised by someone whose opinion matters to us, in some families the topic is too explosive to risk discussing.

Sometimes parents will disagree on the best approach to take, with one avoiding the issue and the other confronting it. Alison admits her marriage has been tested by her children's rejection of faith. She explains, 'It has caused arguments as we have disagreed over how to handle the situation. I have been more willing to take a step back and allow them to come to their own conclusions without any pressure, whereas my husband has been determined not to waste any opportunity to point them in the right direction.' Both feel strongly that it is important to have the right strategy, and fear that the other is doing damage rather than helping.

It is best to acknowledge that this issue does take its toll on relationships, and not just hold our breath and wait for it to pass. Sadly, the worst case scenario – alienation, a fractured and broken family – does sometimes play out. Ingrid's daughter 'rejected God and moved to Thailand'. Chris spent ten years trying to conceal his location from his parents. Kirsty relocated to a city two days' drive from her home town, and didn't speak to her mum or dad for three years.

Jesus tells a story about a son who left his family for a distant country, a story widely known as the parable of the prodigal son (Luke 15:11–32). Unable to contain his impatience for his father to die, the son requested his inheritance and scarpered. There was no texting, no Facebook, no Skype, and if there had been I doubt he would have wanted to stay in touch. After all, what he was doing wouldn't have exactly made daddy proud. Read what you like into 'wild living' – that was what the cash was funding. They were well and truly estranged, he and his father, separated by time, space and culture.

The story doesn't end there. The son comes home. You could use this as a paradigm of a successful outcome, but if you were to study it for lessons in what to do to get your child to come home to God, you would find no pointers. The father does nothing. He doesn't put him under house arrest, but lets him gather together his stuff and head off into the distance. He doesn't track him covertly, just to keep tabs on where he is. He doesn't even wait a while and then send out a search party. He just waits and waits and waits. And is there waiting, champagne on ice, when his heartbreaker of a boy finally shows up. This is a story about our father God, and God is the ultimate father. He is a father who knows what it feels like to see his children walk away without a backward glance, and his compassion for our pain knows no bounds. He feels the same way as we do when our children walk away from our faith. And he's waiting with us for them to come home.

Lovetown or bust

Religious disagreements have caused wars, and they can split families. But they don't have to. We have a choice about how to respond to our children's developing ideologies and thoughts on faith when they diverge from our own. We can choose to fight, we can show them our distress, we can coldly give up hope. Or, we can let them know that we love them, respect them, listen to them with no agenda but that of finding out how they are and communicate our ongoing commitment to them – a non-negotiable commitment.

Becca has come to faith recently, but she says, 'I know with absolute certainty, that if I rejected God my parents would not reject me. They told me over and over again until I was sick of hearing it that they love me no matter what – no matter what I

I know ... they love me no matter what

believe, no matter what I do.' Loving our children in this way is loving them as God loves them, and it is love that will have the last word.

Chapter 2

Parents in pain

Katharine Hill

There are few of us who haven't waited up until the small hours of the morning to deal with an errant teenager who has paid scant regard to a curfew or who has returned having consumed more alcohol than is good for them. Those kinds of issues go with the turf, they are part and parcel of the teenage years and there are books and seminars giving helpful advice to parents on how to deal with these challenges.

For a number of parents, however, these storms are but the early warning signs of an approaching tornado, and life can get tougher still. But even then there is help at hand to navigate the feelings of guilt, frustration, anger, inadequacy and pain that can take a hold of us when our children are in trouble.

This chapter, however, seeks to address a different sort of pain. It is the pain and anguish borne by Christian parents whose children turn their back on the faith they have sought to instil in them from an early age. In this situation our child's decision can be sudden and dramatic or simply the result of a subtle change in priorities over time.

Helena comments: 'My daughter quietly walked away from God at about 16, wanting to live a bit of a party lifestyle. While she was at home she tried to live a double life; she was outwardly compliant and would come to church with us on Sundays, but was unobtrusively living a life that was hedonistic. When she went to university she dropped all pretence of being a Christian. It was a gradual drifting away from all that she had once known to be true.'

Patrick's experience was quite different: 'Alex was helping me change the tyre on the car. It was a Sunday afternoon and I said we should put the tools away as it was time to head off to church. He stood up, looked me in the eye and

I don't believe in that stuff anymore

said, "Dad – I'm not coming. I don't believe in that stuff anymore." I admired his integrity and honesty, but his decision seemed to come from nowhere and has caused us much soul-searching over the years.'

Fault lines

I write this on the anniversary of the devastating earthquake, measuring 9.0 on the Richter Scale, that struck the north eastern coast of Japan in March 2011. The earthquake was one of the most powerful since records began, and was caused as the different plates that make up the Earth's surface moved in opposite directions, eventually breaking and forming a fault. The energy that was released caused the apparently solid and rigid Earth to move, shaking the ground, collapsing buildings and devastating cities.

When children and parents go in opposite directions, there can also be a seismic shift in family dynamics. Strong emotions can simmer under the surface and cause a fault line that can then erupt into an earthquake.

Michelle comments: 'When Naomi told us she didn't believe in God any more we felt helpless. She left home soon afterwards to move in with her boyfriend. As a family we have never been good at discussing difficult issues and lots of things were left unsaid. Ian and I had got into the habit of dealing with things independently and, looking back, it would have been so much better to have talked together about how we were feeling – to acknowledge the pain rather than bury everything beneath the surface.'

There are five common emotions that often converge to cause fault lines to appear and the ground surface to shake.

Rejection

When a child chooses a different path it can be difficult not to take their decision personally and to feel that it is a rejection of who we are. Many young people we interviewed confessed that they delayed telling their parents of their decision because they knew of the deep hurt and disappointment it would cause.

Sue writes: 'I believe that, probably due to my performance-based upbringing, my sense of self-value and feeling accepted was inextricably tied to my performance as a Christian mother in bringing up her sons to be good Christians.'

Megan also explains: 'When the boys were little we tried to do everything we could to build a home with God at the centre. We were involved in the local church, we prayed with them, read Bible stories to them and tried to make a living faith very much a part of family life. I know Elliott has rejected our values and not us, but sometimes it feels as if the two are intertwined – our faith is so much part of our identity.'

Guilt

If the feeling of rejection is common, guilt is the emotion that seems to overwhelm every parent of a prodigal child. Time and again parents look back and ask, 'Where did we go wrong?' In the film *Sliding Doors*, the trajectory of Helen's life is determined in a few seconds by the simple fact of whether or not she catches a train. The film plays out two versions of her life that result from this moment. If Helen catches the train she goes home to find her partner in bed with another woman and leaves him for a different life. On the other hand, if she misses the train she remains ignorant of the affair and her life takes another course altogether.

As parents, we can make the mistake of trying to pinpoint a moment in our family story where life could have taken a different course. We look back, searching for an answer, and think, 'if only...'. If only we had prayed with them/ had read Bible stories to them/hadn't made them go

Where did we go wrong?

to church/had made them go to church/hadn't moved house/had encouraged them to do a different course at university... if only. Our desperation leads us to want to rewrite the script with a different ending.

Perhaps if we can alight on an 'if only' we can at least find someone or something to blame. The only problem is that very often we don't know what we did wrong. The feeling of guilt overwhelms and paralyses us, bringing a sense of failure and hopelessness.

Graham tells his story: 'Ben became a Christian in his teens and spent some time in his gap year working for a mission organisation. He then went to university, joined the Christian Union and continued to be involved in Christian activities. It was when he came home after the first term that everything changed. We noticed his hair, style of clothes and general demeanour were different. A couple of weeks into the holidays, Mary was collecting him from a party and on the way home in the car he said he had something to tell us, but he needed to tell us together when we were home. We sat down in the kitchen and he told us he was gay, and

Grace is not about condoning but loving

he felt therefore he could no longer be a Christian. Homosexuality wasn't something we had really spoken about, but it seemed he had imbibed that way of thinking from our Christian culture. I tried to see if he would change his mind, to see whether he could find a way of returning to his faith, but he was adamant.'

Andy Frost in *Losing Faith* writes, 'The church has become notorious for its lack of grace about homosexuality. Grace is not about condoning but loving.'[1] The issue of homosexuality is not being debated as part of the subject of this book; however, Ben was simply unable to reconcile his homosexual feelings with his Christian faith, and so turned his back on all he had believed in until that point.

Graham continues, 'My overwhelming emotion at the time was one of guilt. As his father I kept going back over the past, over things I had said and done or things I had

---

[1] Andy Frost, *Losing Faith*, Authentic Media, 2010, p52

failed to do, and asking myself, "What did I do wrong?" Has judgmentalism killed my son's faith?'

Rob Parsons writes: 'So many parents are carrying a heavy load of guilt they have no right to bear. That's not to say they have been perfect parents. They have just been *parents* – parents who have given this task their very best effort.'[2]

We all know parents who have broken every rule in the book, but whose children have followed a path any parent would be pleased with. And we know godly parents who have provided warm, secure, Christ-centred homes and yet find that at least one of their children has chosen a different path. We can do our very best as parents, but at the end of the day we have to leave the outcome open. And even if we could have been

God ... too ... knows the ... pain of his children choosing to go their own way

perfect parents – what then? God is our perfect heavenly Father and yet he too knows the anguish, hurt and pain of his children choosing to go their own way.

---

[2] Rob Parsons, *Bringing Home the Prodigals*, Hodder & Stoughton, 2003

Disappointment

As Christian parents we will have an aspiration for our child that we will hold on to tenaciously throughout our lives. This is our deep desire that they will have hearts that respond to God's love and will discover a living faith of their own. The awkward matter of free will means that holding firmly to this hope makes us vulnerable to the very real possibility of crashing disappointment. We are not able to lay down this hope in the same way we can relinquish our hopes for them to become Prime Minister or an international gymnast. There is far more at stake.

Rae and Mike have two sons, Barney and Tim. They spoke of their deep disappointment at seeing Tim leave for university knowing that he had drifted in his faith, but never having had an opportunity to talk to him about it. 'We were feeling desperate. We felt the clock was ticking and that we would have fewer opportunities to talk to him about faith once he had left home. We had a difficult conversation when we tried to tell him that we loved him anyway, even though we were disappointed that he seemed to have put God on hold. At the time it felt like we had made matters worse, but it helped to acknowledge how we were feeling and meant that faith was no longer a taboo subject.'

Proverbs 13:12 says, 'Hope deferred makes the heart sick.' Although it does not ease the pain, it is perhaps comforting to know that disappointment is the natural response to unrealised dreams and unfulfilled hopes.

Shame

Rachel comments: 'When I look at other families with their children in church, the fact that Tom chooses not to come with us makes me feel rubbish. Comments from other parents make me feel like we've messed up in our parenting. We often feel isolated and ashamed.'

> **Comments from other parents make me feel like we've messed up in our parenting**

Many parents will know the extreme discomfort when an issue with a challenging child holds a mirror to their lives and reveals an aspect of their character or an attitude of their heart that they would prefer to have kept well hidden. I can recall a number of occasions when I have been pleased that our children have done well, simply because it has reflected well on me. I remember the warm glow of pride as one of our children reported back on the great things God had done during a mission trip to Uganda. Conversely, when things have not gone according to plan, when one of our children had too much to drink on the church family week away, my first thought was, 'What will the other parents think of me and of my parenting?'

The root of this shame is minding more about others' opinions of us and our parenting than about what God thinks. Note to self: remember the wristband that one of the children used to wear that said 'Audience of One' (for the uninitiated, that means God!).

If we are honest, parents whose children are fully engaged with their faith are encouraged to feel a modicum of pride, whereas those who have at least one child who has chosen a different path can be made to feel they have failed. Society encourages us to measure our significance by our children's achievements, and this way of thinking has subtly invaded the church. We believe (rightly) that family life matters to God, but we sometimes raise the bar so high that 'success' in family becomes an idol in itself. We judge each other by how well our children are doing spiritually, and parents of children who are not engaged with church are left feeling that they are second class, or haven't quite made the grade.

A few years ago I remember hearing a mother of three children who are all pursuing God with every fibre of their being say, 'If any of my children lost their faith I would feel I had completely failed as a mother.' I am sure she did not mean to cause offence, but how could she not have known that every mother in the room longed more than anything for their children to be following Jesus? Did she really think that her children's response to God was a direct result of her parenting? If I had been in her shoes I may have been tempted to feel the same, but that kind of attitude does little to assuage the very real pain of parents who have sowed as hard and prayed as hard as she did, but for the time being have not seen any harvest.

Graham and Mary continue their story: 'One evening shortly after Ben told us he was gay and was no longer a Christian, our teenage daughter came into the living room and asked us to turn off the television as she had something to tell us. She told us she was pregnant and the father of the baby was her 17-year-old boyfriend. We felt devastated, shocked and ashamed; this went against everything our family stood for and believed in. Following the pregnancy her young faith dwindled and she drifted away from the church. It was a traumatic time for us.'

Fear

Where there is guilt and shame, fear is often close behind. Instead of rewinding the story and thinking 'if only', sometimes we can look at the choices our children are making and fast forward and ask 'what if?' The possible answers to some of those questions can grip us with fear.

Ella writes: 'As a mother I used to imagine the worst and play over in my mind awful scenarios of things that could happen to my boys. One day, while on holiday, I made the decision not to think like that anymore. Instead I chose to imagine a different future and to believe that God had the power to turn things around. Gradually I found that my overwhelming sense of fear began to be replaced

There was nothing that could separate us from God's love

with a quiet confidence that whatever happened, there was nothing that could separate us from God's love.'

Guy and Margaret's deepest fear, shared by many parents, is the thought that they might not be with their children in heaven: 'Of course we want them to live life to the full now, but it's the thought of a possible eternity without them that, on a bad day, fills us with fear and on a good day spurs us on to pray.'

The Valley of Achor

As parents these five fault lines – rejection, guilt, disappointment, shame and fear – can converge to shake our foundations to the core. But although we don't have the power to stop the tremors happening in the first place, there are things we can do to strengthen the foundations and to reduce the impact.

Knowing we are not alone, that there are other parents walking a similar path, can sometimes be all that is needed to restore our perspective. At Care for the Family we are reminded of this principle time and again. Just knowing that there are others who can come alongside us, who have experienced the same issues and who understand can give us hope.

If we are feeling rejection, guilt, disappointment, shame or fear, we can choose to stand on the truth of God's Word and recognise that those negative emotions have no place in his purposes for us or for our families. We can ask God to show us the root of our feelings and to expose where there have been legitimate issues that may have contributed to our child's decision. And we can ask him to show us where our feelings are founded on mistaken beliefs. As we bring our pain to the cross, we will find that God will have compassion on us. With open arms he offers acceptance instead of rejection, freedom instead of guilt, hope instead of disappointment, confidence instead of shame and courage instead of fear.

Paul writes in his letter to the Romans, '... we also glory in our sufferings, because we know that suffering produces perseverance; perseverance, character; and character, hope. And hope does not put us to shame, because God's love has been poured out into our hearts through the Holy Spirit, who has been given to us' (Romans 5:3–5).

Paul himself knew physical suffering; he was imprisoned, shipwrecked, hungry, thirsty, cold and naked. He also knew something of the pain and disappointment of seeing those he loved choose a different path. In his letter to Timothy he writes about his fellow worker Demas who 'loved this world' and deserted him (2 Timothy 4:10). And it is in this context that he encourages us to rejoice not *because* of but *in* our suffering, because he knows it is not meaningless. Part of God's purpose is to produce character in his children. Many families walking this painful journey can testify to the character that has grown through these testing times.

Graham and Mary, who have had to cope with more than most, comment: 'We would never have chosen this path; it continues to be a roller-coaster, but God has used it. We have no end of Christian parents coming to talk to us when their child has lost their faith and is in trouble. There are no magic answers but we can offer empathy, a listening ear and hope. They know they are not alone. We have been tempted to look back and ask "Why us?", but we are learning that that's not the right question to ask. There are things we don't understand, but we have learnt to trust God with our children day by day.' I know Graham and Mary and I can testify to the wonderful work God has done in their lives. In and through their suffering they radiate the goodness of God.

We have learnt to trust God with our children day by day

I met up with an old friend recently who told me about the painful journey he has walked with two of his children who have been far from God. He said, 'Since they turned away from God, I've not been able to sing. It's the grit in the oyster of my life that is producing a pearl.' He then went on to ask me if I had seen the film *Amazing Grace*, and reminded me of a particular scene. While Wilberforce is engaged in his life's battle for the abolition of slavery, he turns to his friend and says, 'I haven't been able to sing for twenty years.' My friend continued, 'Most people miss that in the film, but I know what it means. When we have known pain we sometimes have to live with the consequences – Jacob walked with a limp for the rest of his life. My walk with God is close, but I have known pain and I can't sing through it.'

In Hosea 2 God promises his people that he will '… make the Valley of Achor a door of hope. There [they] will sing as in the days of [their] youth' (Hosea 2:15). As parents this can be our prayer. Just as the Israelites experienced a time of great suffering and despair in the Valley of Achor, we can pray that God will be with us in our pain and that he will journey with us through our desolate valley. And, as we move forward, we can ask that he will once again put a song in our hearts and give us renewed hope as we trust our children, who have been his children all along, to him, their heavenly Father.

Chapter 3

As for me ... no thanks

Jo Swinney

Do we really want to know why our sons don't believe in God, or why our daughters won't come to church with us? I think, quite understandably, many of us don't want to hear what's actually going on out of a sense of fear. We don't want the shreds of hope we clutch pulled away from us, or perhaps it would make us hopping mad to realise how little of the spiritual seed we have sown has germinated. And our adult children are avoiding these conversations too; they don't want a messy confrontation, they don't want to see the hurt and disappointment in their parents' eyes, they maybe don't really know what they think and don't want to be shoehorned into a small atheistic box. Perhaps this chapter could be a starting point for a dialogue between you. It could be that some of the stories here resonate with your own, or perhaps they will stir a curiosity in you to find out if any of the causes of doubt in them ring true for your child. Everyone has their own reasons for finding themselves where they are. Here are some of the reasons I have heard while researching *Keeping Faith*:

Too much pressure

Wild animals will respond in different ways if they feel trapped. A hedgehog will roll quietly into a ball, a cat will stand on tiptoe and bristle out its fur to try and look bigger and more intimidating, a rattlesnake will rattle a warning and get ready to attack. People also respond in different ways if they feel trapped, but the basic idea behind the reaction is to escape. Trying to force faith down a person's throat inevitably backfires.

Kirsty's sister and brother are Christians, but she is not. A typical weekday in their childhood would begin with prayers before breakfast, followed by a Bible reading and devotional. They would then head off to their Christian school, and return home for more prayers and devotionals around dinner. They read through the entire Bible three or four times as a family project. On Sundays there was Sunday School, followed by church, an afternoon at someone's house ('visiting and witnessing') or having guests at their house and, since it was the Lord's Day, no sports or non-spiritual entertainment.

Christian everything, all the time, baby!

In addition to these routines, there were missionary trips, witnessing on the streets, singing hymns in nursing homes, reading a million books about missionaries/martyrs/Christians/theology – as she puts it, 'Christian everything, all the time, baby.' Kirsty remembers acute frustration that she had no choice in how she spent her time, let alone what she thought. Part of the issue was that she felt enveloped in this stifling Christian culture until the moment she fled not only her home but her home town and put the Canadian prairies between them.

There is a natural and necessary developmental stage, usually between the ages of 11 and 13, where children begin to question the values and world view passed on to them by their parents, where they separate their identity from that of their parents and begin to form a sense of self as an autonomous being. It is at this point that Christian parents become very anxious, because their child will quite possibly want to give all the Christian teaching they have received throughout childhood a great deal of critical scrutiny. The very worst thing to do at this juncture is to panic and try to prevent them escaping. At best, they will put up a façade of religiosity to keep you happy. This was Alfie's choice: 'When I was growing up I was taught that Christianity was true; it was on a par with gravity. Church was not an option, and when I stopped wanting to go it caused rows and in the end it was easier to go than to face the guilt of not

Church was not an option, and when I stopped wanting to go it caused rows doing what my parents wanted. I continued to go for another seven years, even professing faith because this was the way things were set out in my family and that was what was expected of me.' I'm sure what Alfie's parents really longed for was for their son to know and love Jesus, but what they got was a short-lived pretence to keep them off his back.

A negative experience of church

Church attendance is often the first point of conflict when it comes to someone working out matters of faith for themselves, and I can't help but wonder if perhaps it has been given too much significance as a marker of a person's inner commitments. I am not trying to imply that it isn't vital for a Christian to belong to a wider family of fellow believers, but rather suggesting that by making this the mast to which colours must be nailed, we deflect the heart of the matter: have they been introduced to Jesus and what did they make of him if they have? A bit further down the line, they will most likely want to search out fellow followers. The problem is that, for many people, disenchantment with faith begins with disenchantment with a particular church, and no one explains to them that one doesn't have to lead to the other.

Why do teenagers often push against church? There are a myriad of explanations. They have no one there of their own age, or no one they particularly get on with anyway. They have competing commitments, perhaps related to sport. They are busy trying to find a way to get under their parents' skin, because that's what some teenagers like doing. They see the mess church members and leaders get themselves into from time to time, and they

Making church a battle to the death is not the wisest approach

become disillusioned and cynical. Or, more benignly, they just dislike the music and find the teaching boring. They have been up late the night before and want to catch up on sleep.

Some may feel church is absorbing their parents' attention and depriving them of a family life. Lara's parents became Christians when she was a teenager, and since then she feels church has almost swallowed them up. Now she is a mother of two and resents the fact that she and her children see so little of them. She told me with some bitterness in her voice that, 'Family should be more important than anything else, but with my parents church comes before the grandchildren. They live locally but they don't see us that often because they're so busy with church stuff. They can't even come on holiday with us unless it's between Monday and Saturday. We've tried to talk about it with them, but nothing changes.'

If this was a form with a space saying 'any other:' I'm sure you could fill it. Even mature, godly, seasoned Christians find church a challenge sometimes. Making church a battle to the death is not the wisest approach to keeping someone in touch with God.

Friends and romantic relationships

Very few people have a coherent conversion to atheism. More likely is a gradual drift downstream, along with other drifters whose company they enjoy. Either this is a group of friends or, more frequently, a romantic relationship. If the person they fall for is not a Christian, and their Christian roots haven't yet grown deep or strong, it may stop them growing. It isn't only the issue of having sex that may cause a problem, it is the desire we all have to mesh our lives with the people we love, to share a common outlook, to smooth over areas of potential conflict. I know from personal experience how hard it is to stay spiritually healthy in those circumstances.

Nat and Helena write, 'Our third daughter, Tabitha, got involved with a guy in the church when she was 16. After a couple of years, he walked away from God and our daughter went with him. Although the relationship ended soon afterwards, she did not reconnect with God. She then met her current partner, a great young man but not a Christian, and she has lived with him and by his values ever since.' It seems, and it is, constraining for a young person to restrict potential boyfriends or girlfriends to fellow believers, and it takes a resolute commitment to God to make that sacrifice. This is one of the major hazards that those raised in a Christian home must navigate in finding a genuine faith of their own.

Questions and badly-handled questioning

Questioning received wisdom is good and healthy; belief that doesn't stand up to a rigorous probe is more akin to superstition. But having the foundations we have built life on scrutinised by critical eyes is not easy, and we may be fearful of what cracks might be exposed. Teenagers in particular can sense when they are being deflected, or if there is any hint of hypocrisy. If their questions are shut down, they will wonder if it is because there just isn't a good enough answer.

I've not managed to get any of my head-based questions answered

Andrew, a self-professed apostate in his late twenties, describes his journey thus far: 'I lost my faith when I started university on being challenged to question my beliefs.

In more recent years I've had many conversations with Christians. I've not managed to get any of my head-based questions answered, and it seems that the only important thing is the experience of God.'

There is an element of 'foolishness' in devotion to Christ (1 Corinthians 1:21), yet it doesn't demand a reckless abandonment of rationality. The apostle Peter writes, 'Always be prepared to give an answer to everyone who asks you to give the reason for the hope that you have' (1 Peter 3:15). Indeed, there is a whole discipline devoted to furnishing us with reasons – apologetics. Questions are inevitable. Losing belief as a result of the answers or lack thereof, is not. One of the keys here is acknowledging the complexity of the issues. If we aren't prepared for

Sometimes what people are rejecting is the way God has been represented to them

other viewpoints, they are going to shock us when we encounter them. Like Andrew, John was shaken by his time at university: 'I was exposed to new philosophical questions – and answers. Only the answers were not from God: apparently there could be other ways of explaining things! Ninety per cent of the books at home were from an evangelical Christian perspective. I hadn't come across other ideas before.'

Bad examples of Christians you know well

When people seem to 'reject God', sometimes what they are rejecting is the way God has been represented to them – perhaps a representation that any sane person would find repellent. They may not see that religion has made any sort of positive impact on those who profess it, and they conclude they are better off without it. Lara observes that, 'Most of my mum's worries are about not being a good enough Christian.'

Kylie remembers, 'My parents didn't really speak about having a relationship with God or their faith in day-to-day life. It was something I knew they had and that's why we attended some kind of church function around four times a week. But they never spoke about the benefits of being a Christian and the personal effect it had on their lives.' Her parents' faith didn't prevent her father from sexually abusing her sister, or her mother's emotional neglect.

Steve's youth leader's marriage fell apart when both he and his wife began relationships with other married people in the church – three marriages destroyed in one fell swoop.

The flip side of this is the power of growing up in a home where Christ impacts the atmosphere and the very fabric of the family in a life-giving sense. Even if someone still chooses not to be a Christian, perhaps because it is incompatible with the lifestyle they want to pursue, they can never fully deny the reality of what they have seen.

Gavin Calver's parents left for the United States when he was 17, following what they described as a clear 'call from God', despite his ultimatum that if they went he wouldn't live another day as a Christian. Later, writing about his subsequent conversion, he says, 'The example of my parents played a huge part in this. They'd shown me that this Jesus thing mattered and that you gave up anything and everything in order to serve him fully. They loved me dearly, but they lived for Jesus with everything they had. I never really knew what it meant to love Jesus until my parents left me for him.'[3]

No personal encounter with God

Some people have just never had a personal encounter with God, and therefore have no reason other than loyalty or nostalgia to maintain links with Christianity.

This encounter is not something a parent can manufacture so any sense of responsibility for whether it happened or not is misplaced.

Life events make you reassess

Gail had positive experiences of church, saw an authentic

---

[3] *Disappointed with Jesus?* Monarch, 2004, p125

expression of faith in her parents' lives, felt the freedom to explore and challenge belief and even recalls having what she refers to as 'nature-mystical experiences', which she had no problem reconciling with a Christian framework. She relates what happened to turn her off God like this: 'My parents sold the family home without telling us children until a week before we had to move, which was a huge breach of trust. Six months later my grandmother died, the first time I had experienced close bereavement. Almost immediately after that I lost my faith – it was within about a fortnight. The problems of existence no longer seemed to have any acceptable answers.' Gail had come up against what has been called 'the problem of pain', and the problem suffocated her belief in a good God.

Susie went through a particularly messy divorce eight years ago. Each family will cope in their own way with this situation. Susie says of her own experience, 'Without a doubt, our marriage breakup and their father leaving affected all of our three children's faith. They all handled it differently, but it seemed toughest for Lauren who was 12 at the time. I think she felt badly let down by God and was very angry. She gradually grew more and more disillusioned and, when she believed in him at all, she felt he'd abandoned her.'

In the parable of the sower (Luke 8:4–15), some seed falls on rocks and some lands among thorns. Jesus explains that this represents those who have heard the word, 'but in the time of testing they fall away' and those who 'are choked by life's worries'. He knew how hard it can be for the seed of God's Word to take root and that, for some people, the difficulties thrown up by life would be too much.

Unintended consequences

There are various ways we can respond as parents when our children are not doing what we want them to do, which change as they grow older. Very small children can be physically moved into place. Toddlers can be put in disgrace on the bottom step (with nothing to keep them there but the mystical force field of parental willpower). Preschoolers can be corralled by a system of reward and punishment, and older children discover consequences for themselves. Later on, it is tempting to try to keep a semblance of control or at least influence, but our tactics become sneakier. We may think we are just nudging them in a good direction, but some well-meaning and innocently executed actions can be interpreted by our children in ways that might surprise us. This may be hard to hear, but if we can see ourselves from their perspective, it might help us understand why alienation can occur despite our very best intentions.

Books

In place of an open discussion about an area that might have been sealed off as too toxic to enter, a Christian book is quietly left by the bed or wings its way through the post. While Holly thinks it is sweet that her parents are still trying in a roundabout way to get through to her, her sister Charlotte receives the books as a personal attack. It is worth just giving careful thought to how well received this might be as a gesture.

Conversation

Keeping God in the room by steering conversations to spiritual topics, however tangential the connection, can make people feel it isn't possible to have any genuine interactions with their family. They get the impression that we have no interest in anything about their lives other than the state of their soul, and that they are being manipulated into stuffy corners of debate rather than enjoying a good chat.

Prayer

Enlisting others to pray about a situation makes total sense to Christians. To get as many people praying as you can if you believe there is a God who hears what you say, cares about it and can do something in response is logical. To someone who doesn't hold that view, it represents a breach of confidentiality, a pious gossip session and all kinds of people you don't know concerned with personal matters you hadn't chosen to share. Lara puts it this way: 'Sometimes when I have confided in my mum she's told everyone in her church to get them to pray about it, but then they all know my business. It makes me feel betrayed.' Perhaps what we need to hear here is to respect their boundaries, and exercise discretion and restraint in who we ask to pray for our children.

> **Sometimes when I have confided in my mum she's told everyone in her church**

Bible verses

Quoting the Bible to others when they need comfort or support is a valid thing to do for someone who sees the Bible as you do, but may not be received well by someone who doesn't value it. Kirsty emailed me a rather cynical example of a typical exchange she has had repeatedly over the years with her mum and dad:

Kid: Hi parent, I'm having a hard time thinking about this or that question, or having this or that experience. Can you give me some guidance or comfort or just plain company?

Parent: Well kiddo, here's a verse for you, and another verse, and here's a prayer, and why don't you pray some more about it?

Kid: Ummmm... I was trying to tell you something important and now you're quoting Bible verses at me. I guess I won't try that again.

Parent: Here's another verse! And we're praying for you. Oh and did you get that card I sent you in the mail, with the story of that woman who was living in [pick your country and decade] and was having a hard time with [pick a problem] and then a minister came and prayed with her and told her about [pick a psalm] and how she was so comforted by this intangible poem written thousands of years ago in another culture that has nothing in common whatsoever with the way we live now? Wait, why are you so sad and walking away from me?

Apologising

While we should always say sorry to our children for specific things we haven't got right, or ways we've hurt them, implying in a general sense that we have failed as parents suggests they haven't turned out as we had hoped. Josh remembers that his dad,

I felt he was saying I'd turned out badly

'...would often apologise for getting his parenting wrong, and would ask us what he'd done. I felt he was saying I'd turned out badly.' No one wants to feel that who they are reflects poorly on their parents' ability to raise a child. It doesn't take a huge leap of imagination to realise how that sounds to your offspring.

Keeping God in the room, enlisting prayer support, giving out helpful Bible verses and apologising when we have gone wrong are all good things to do in principle, and I don't mean to say that we should never do them. But I do think we would do well to consider how, when and why we do them, whether the impact is going to be positive or negative and how the gesture is likely to be received.

Good to talk

Conversations about faith with someone you disagree with can be fraught, but they don't have to be. We all appreciate being listened to, and if we let our defences down, we will probably find areas of agreement to explore. Who

... it isn't all about us

hasn't had their faith rocked when things go wrong? Haven't most of us struggled with church at some point, or been tempted to do things that we know we really shouldn't? As parents, we can obviously help or hinder our children's faith journeys, but it isn't all about us. Far from it.

Chapter 4

Mapping the borders

Katharine Hill

Saturday 3 September 1988 was a red letter day in our household. It was the day our first child was born – an anniversary we later discovered he shared with Oliver Cromwell and the outbreak of World War Two. The next couple of days were a haze of broken nights, breastfeeding, dirty nappies and visitors. Just a week before I had been working in an office as a lawyer, and the early arrival of George Thomas Hill turned my orderly life upside down. I felt completely overwhelmed by the realisation that I was totally responsible for this new baby – who was soon to demonstrate that he had a mind of his own – and yet I hadn't a clue what I was doing.

In an attempt to equip myself for the task, I tried to lay my hands on as many parenting books as possible. I remember that one likened parenting to windsurfing. The only way to learn, it said, was to make mistakes in public.

Another book proffered by an earnest visitor was called *Making Little Christians*. I had precious few minutes to myself but tried to seize them when they came, and reading this book became a priority. I was desperate to do the right thing, and to be the kind of parent that brought her children up to love Jesus, and this book seemed to offer the recipe. If I followed the instructions, all would be well.

The arrival of a new baby brings a huge sense of responsibility, but as well as taking care of their physical and emotional needs parents have responsibility for their child's spiritual development. The Bible tells us that we are stewards of creation, and that includes our children; they are a gift from God for us to care for. But we must not, and cannot, assume total responsibility for their relationship with the one who gave them life in the first place.

There are, of course, important things we can do at different stages to encourage faith in our children and build strong foundations in their lives. It is said that 'faith is more often caught than taught'. As parents we have an opportunity to teach our children about God, to pass on values and live lives in a way that makes it easier than not for our children to love him. But we can only lead them so far. Each of us needs to discover a faith of our own and not one that has simply been inherited from our parents.

As parents we play an important role in helping our children through the initial stages of faith, helping them arrive at the place where they can choose for themselves whether or not they believe this Jesus is worth following for the rest of their lives.

But there are no guarantees about what will happen when our children begin to make up their own minds. What if they ask questions and yet are unable to find answers that satisfy their doubts? What if, with honesty and integrity, they decide the Christian faith is not for them? What then? As parents how should we respond? How do we live in the tension of their decision and still leave the door wide open for them? Where do the boundaries lie?

Navigating our relationship with a child who has decided on a different direction of life than we had hoped for can be like traversing a minefield. Certain courses of action will disturb the surface and cause an explosion, whereas others will enable us to continue to make progress, keeping the family relationships strong. Whatever the situation, we would be wise to proceed with caution.

Over the years as I have spoken with thousands of parents, many have shared lessons of things they have learnt, often the hard way. Here are some dos and don'ts that might be helpful.

Don't control

In our desperation for our children to find a faith of their own, we can sometimes become heavy-handed and controlling. We can't bear to think that they might choose a different path and so, to protect everyone, we try to live their faith for them and dictate the outcome.

When our children are little we control most aspects of their lives and do everything for them. We have to. We decide what they eat and when, what they wear, when they go to bed. We tie their shoelaces and wipe runny noses. We choose which Bible stories to tell them, we pray with them and for them, we take them to church, enlist them in the holiday club, take them to Christian festivals. We are in control. There are challenges, but at the end of the day we call the tune. However, as time moves on and our children enter the teenage years, in all aspects of our parenting things need to change. Youth pastor Daniel Hahn writes about this transition:

... as kids grow up ... Our best shot is influence ...[4]

'Parents face two options. We can keep using the same patterns we used when they were young (and frustrate ourselves to death), or we can realize that our methods must change as our kids develop. As hard as it is our role must move from controller to consultant. What do consultants do? They ask questions, offer opinions, share experiences, present options and forecast outcomes. Ultimately, however, they step back and allow the client to make decisions. Consultants understand what they can and cannot do for their client, and as result the client owns the process as well as the results. The fact is, as kids grow up we can't control much of what they do anyhow. Our best shot is influence ... "[4]

Some parents fail to make this adjustment and seek to control their children well into adulthood. Such parents – whose style has come to be known as 'helicopter parenting' – hover over every aspect of their adult children's lives, exerting inappropriate control and impeding independence. Letting our children go is undoubtedly one of the hardest parts of parenting, but we do our children no favours if we keep them tied to our apron strings and prevent them from becoming the men and women they were created to be.

Letting our children go is one of the hardest parts of parenting

The role of consultant is relatively straightforward when the client takes our advice, and it can be rewarding to watch our young adult child take decisions that we have steered them towards and that we know are for their good. The only problem, however, with being the consultant is

[4] Daniel Hahn, *Teaching Your Kids the Truth About Consequences* Bethany House Publishers, 1995, p21

that the client is also free to ignore our advice. It can be frustrating to watch our children disregard our wisdom and make what we may consider poor decisions over issues of lifestyle, finance, friendships or career plans. More painful still is to stand back as they reject the faith that we hoped to share. It's then that we need to remind ourselves that we are the consultants; we can do so much, but we can only do so much.

Don't manipulate

There won't be many parents of children who leave home for the first time who haven't sought to help God along a bit in keeping their children on the straight and narrow. A friend who works for a university mission organisation tells me that in the summer months she is inundated with emails from anxious parents asking if leaders of the Christian Union could make contact with their offspring in the first weeks of term. Two of my children are currently at university and I confess to having made contact with friends, or friends of friends, to ask them if they would invite my children for Sunday lunch (preferably with a rendezvous after the morning service to encourage them to make an appearance). One lunch never got off the ground as the child in question had no desire to meet with a stranger and so never replied to any texts. The other lunch did at least take place, but wasn't repeated. When our third child goes to university this autumn everything in me will want to 'fix' it again – to make sure he doesn't fall through the net – but I will try to take my own advice and resist the urge to manipulate him into the kingdom.

Although these parental endeavours come from the best of motives, and often do pay dividends, I have come to realise that, from my children's perspective, my scheming has been more transparent than I had hoped. My prayers are essential, but the maker of the universe is more than able to arrange events so my children come to a deeper knowledge of him – and he can probably do it without my unwarranted intervention.

Don't pressurise

Saturday morning breakfasts were a special family occasion for Phil, Jackie and their three children. Each Saturday morning Phil would put on an apron and cook a big fry-up and then, after breakfast, they would spend some time praying together as a family. Saturday mornings were sacred; no one would invite friends round or arrange any other activity until after lunch. However, when their middle daughter Ellie went to sixth-form college they noticed she was taking a back seat in the family prayer times. They ignored it initially, but then began to make an issue of it. She would often be out late on a Friday night and then would struggle to get up in the morning. The rest of the family would be waiting, bacon and eggs would be going cold and after much nagging she would eventually make an appearance.

'Saturday mornings had been so special, and it felt like Ellie was spoiling everything by opting out,' Jackie said. 'I didn't want things to change, so I put huge pressure on her to get up and to join in. But looking back I realise I got this so wrong.'

Ellie explained how she felt: 'I wanted a lie-in on a Saturday; I didn't really enjoy the organised praying. Mum assumed I was about to give up on God altogether. She put so much pressure on me, nagging me to get up and to be there, that it had the opposite effect and made me want to opt out completely. If there had been less pressure I might have made more of an effort.'

If there had been less pressure I might have made more of an effort

Don't make faith a battle ground

In trying to find a logical explanation for why our children have decided to opt out of faith we may decide to try the tack of presenting the evidence and arguing them into the kingdom. Although healthy family discussions are to be encouraged, because of the high stakes involved it is very easy for the debate to become emotive and for faith to become a battleground.

Kofi and Diane write about their experience: 'Our willingness to discuss things openly with Paul turned into an excuse for him to argue, criticise and rant at us concerning our faith. We could not talk about God or about church in front of him without an argument. Things were always tense when he was around at home. He needed to know that his attitude wasn't going

We could not talk about God without an argument

to shake us. He still claims to be an atheist, but we continue to discuss with him, when he wants to, the differences in our standpoints.'

Gina stopped going to church when she went to university. She explained that her parents' openness to listen and value her point of view has enabled them to grow closer as a family. 'We are a family that has always had good debates about things, especially around the meal table. What has been important for me is that although Dad makes his point, he also seems to respect what I have to say as well. It means that God can come into the conversation without it becoming an argument.'

Do give space

If our children are to find a faith of their own, it is vital that we give them space.

John's parents' violent reaction to his decision to move in with his girlfriend had the effect of him putting his faith on hold, and resulted in a total breakdown of communication between them. 'For the years that followed I tried to keep my parents out of my life, doing my best to stop them knowing where I lived and worked. They kept pursuing me, and I felt hunted.' John has now come back to faith. Although he knows that his parents' reaction was because they loved him, looking back he wonders if things would have been different if his parents had given him the space to learn some lessons the hard way.

Helen stopped going to church as a teenager. She writes: 'I used to spend Sundays going into London, to Camden and Covent Garden. They seemed vibrant, colourful and full of life in contrast to church, which to me was grey and claustrophobic. My parents never put pressure on me to change my decision and I really think that if they had I wouldn't have come back. It was something I needed to do and it was an important part of my journey. I found out afterwards that they had been horribly worried about me and had been praying their hearts out.'

Do show acceptance

Will and Annie's son Christopher stopped going to the church youth group when he was in the sixth form, while his siblings carried on attending. Will explains: 'We weren't very good at hiding our feelings from him. Chris had grown up in the church and he knew how important our faith was to us, so he didn't really need us to tell him how we felt. It was hard to let it go and so we would make the odd comment in the hope that he might reconsider. In hindsight, it had the opposite effect as I think he felt judged, and that built up a wall between us.'

I think he felt judged, and that built up a wall between us

Tamsin writes about her reaction when her son Seth told her he no longer had a faith. 'At first I felt devastated. I felt like having nothing to do with him, turning my back on him or running away from the situation. However, I read once again the story of the prodigal son and I realised that God's way would be to wait expectantly for his child to come to his senses and that he wouldn't recriminate, criticise, blame, scold or judge.'

We would be foolish to think that we need to point out our disappointment that our adult children have chosen a different path. They know that too well, which often makes their decision more difficult for them. As hard as it can sometimes be, the vital ingredient is to show our children unconditional love and acceptance, while holding in tension our deepest desire for things to be different.

We can look to God as our example. He calls us to love

our children in the way he loves us. He loves us as we are, he sees our hearts and accepts us as we are – but he loves us too much to leave us as we are.

Do encourage contact with people of influence

One of our teenagers spends every Friday after school in a local coffee shop with a very large de luxe hot chocolate, chatting to one of the youth leaders who has become a friend and mentor to him. I have no idea what they talk about, and any probing I have done has been assiduously ignored. And that is how it should be. It is said that it takes a village to raise a child, and as parents we would do well to enlist the support of others in our parenting; in this important task we need all the help we can get. Since our children were very young we have prayed that God would provide people who would be great role models for them. We have asked God to put across their path men and women of character and faith who would invest in them and point them in the right direction. And we are grateful to God for the times when he has answered that prayer. When they were younger we would seek these people out and invite them round to our home. Now our children are older we continue to pray that people of influence would come into their lives. Grandparents, members of the wider family and work colleagues can often speak a word of wisdom that our children might just filter out when hearing it from us.

Do leave the door open

Leah put her faith on hold while at university but has recently started coming back to church. Her advice to parents is: 'Always keep the door open for your children.'

Rae and Mike would pray with their son Barney before he went back to university, but didn't do so for his brother Tim 'because we felt he wouldn't want it and it would be imposing on him'. Rae explained: 'As Barney was leaving to go back to

Always keep the door open for your children

university, we sat down to pray with him and I instinctively stood up to close the door. Barney challenged me to keep it open and not to shut Tim out. With that, Tim came in and sat on the arm of the chair in the doorway – and, to our delight and amazement, joined in our prayers.'

The door is never shut, and as parents we need to be careful not to trap our children in a room they are simply passing through.

In this journey we can resist the temptation to manipulate or control, we can surround our children with mentors and we can give them freedom and space to decide for themselves, but all this will have no power if we aren't on our knees praying for them. Prayer is what is really going to make the difference – and that's why we have given the entire next chapter to it.

Chapter 5

Ask

Katharine Hill

Country music wouldn't usually be my first choice, but while on a car journey recently the words of a country song grabbed my attention. The song 'Angel Hands' beautifully captures the heart of the issues we are seeking to explore. I found myself profoundly moved as the lyrics describe a mother's utter sense of powerlessness while watching her son ruin his life through the bad choices he makes. The refrain expresses her desperation: 'I bet it gets so quiet in heaven sometimes. Even God cries when an angel's hands are tied.'[5]

Many of us will have known that same feeling of helplessness as we have stood by and watched our children turn at the crossroads to take a different path than the one we had hoped for them. But although the choice remains theirs, the truth is that we are neither helpless nor

---

[5] Rodney Atkins, 'Angel Hands'

powerless. We do not have to wait, passively wringing our hands in despair, because we have at our disposal the power of prayer. We can run to our heavenly Father, who longs for our children to come to know him, and pray for them to return home. St Teresa of Avila said, 'You pay God a compliment by asking great things of him,' and what greater thing can we ask God than for his children to know and love him?

The prophet Ezekiel wrote, 'I looked for someone among them … who would stand before me in the gap on behalf of the land …' (Ezekiel 22:30). This is the heart of intercession – to be a go-between, to stand in the gap for another. In the original Greek, 'intercession' meant to have freedom of access in the sense of entering the king's presence to make a request. We don't have to bribe our way in, or, once in, twist God's arm to overcome his reluctance to help us. We have access through Jesus to the very throne room of heaven, and we can come knowing that he delights in our request. We can '… approach God's throne of grace with confidence, so that we may receive mercy and find grace to help us in our time of need' (Hebrews 4:16).

Prayer can move mountains, change the course of history, bring down governments, restore nations, soften hearts, rebuild families, untie hands and bring prodigals home. So how can we pray?

Pray with focus

There isn't a parent who hasn't, at some time, felt anxious about their children, but for some parents the challenge of their children's circumstances can feel overwhelming. The sight of Goliath of Gath, nine feet tall, dressed head to toe in bronze armour, with javelin, sword and spear, would have seemed overwhelming to the most experienced army officer of the day. But David the shepherd boy was able to defeat him with a sling and a pebble, simply because he focused on God and not on the giant before him.

For some parents the challenge of their children's circumstances can feel overwhelming

As we pray for our children, we need to focus not on the giants before us, as intimidating as they may feel, but adjust our gaze to the one to whom we pray, and remind ourselves that as we pray 'the battle is the LORD's' (1 Samuel 17:47). As we do that, we will find that our perspective will change.

Ewan and Jacquie recently found faith for themselves and are parents to adult children Rhiannon, Craig and Tim. They would love to rewind the years and to have the opportunity of sharing their faith with their children. But they comment: 'Although we can't do that, we can pray. We can focus on God and trust that he will show them their need of him (and ours too). Hopefully, we are making up for lost time!'

Pray with persistence

Many of us may have prayed confident prayers of faith for our children when they were young. Years later, however, when those prayers seem to have fallen on deaf ears and show no sign of being answered, we can become weary and be tempted to lose heart and resign ourselves to the status quo. Brian has been praying for his sons Stuart and Michael for many years. He comments, 'At times I have been tempted to give up, but I do not believe for one minute God is finished with either of our sons. Our part is to pray.'

Jesus tells the story of the persistent widow who won't take no for an answer to remind us we 'should always pray and not give up' (Luke 18:1–8). Because of her persistence, the unjust judge 'who neither feared God nor cared what people thought' settles her case. If we approach God with the same boldness, how much more will he, who is just and merciful, want to hear and answer our prayers.

Ella and Paul have four children, two boys and two girls. She recalls: 'I remember being on holiday and saying to God, "I want my boys back." I committed to pray for them in earnest for six weeks. The girls were faithful in praying as well. The story was not straightforward, but five years later both boys have found a faith of their own.'

At the age of 16, St Augustine was living a life far from God. He was unmarried, had fathered a child and joined a heretical group. Monica his mother persisted in prayer for him for 19 years, often coming before God and weeping for her son. In desperation she asked a bishop to speak to Augustine. The bishop refused her request, but said to her, 'Leave him alone for a time … only pray to God for him … Go thy way, and God bless thee, for it is not possible that the son of these tears should perish.' Having prayed passionately for many years, Monica lived to see her son come back to God. He went on to become one of the leading bishops in the fourth century.

Pray with tears

Several years ago I sat at the back of a large auditorium at a Christian summer festival. The speaker had given a powerful talk to a large group of women on the importance of praying for our children. Her talk was both moving and challenging, but it was what happened next that had such impact. She asked

Many were weeping for their children

mothers whose children were far from God to come to the front. Literally hundreds of faithful women came out of their seats, filling the area in front of the stage and back up the aisles. Many were weeping for their children. With many tears these mothers committed to continue to pray and not to give up. I was reminded of the wonderful verse in the psalms where David asks God to put 'my tears in your bottle' (Psalm 56:8, CEV). This refers to an ancient custom of putting precious tears that had been shed in mourning into a small phial which would be placed in the tomb of the person who had died. In the same way as he said to King Hezekiah, God says to us, 'I have heard your prayer and seen your tears' (2 Kings 20:5). Our tears are precious to him; not a single drop is wasted, not a single drop.

Graham and Mary write: 'Our testimony is that the crises in our family have driven us to pray, often with many tears. Without prayer there is no power, but situations like ours force us to come to God because we have run out of our own resources.'

Pray in expectation

Just over a year ago we celebrated with friends as they adopted a beautiful little girl from Ethiopia, after ten long years of waiting; yesterday we received news that the necessary permission has been given for them to adopt a second child. They should receive an email sometime during the next few weeks that will match them with a baby. They are waiting expectantly – checking their inbox three or four times a day – just in case the news has come that they can jump on a plane to meet their son or daughter and bring them home. And that is how we are to wait – not passively, but in expectant hope of the good news of our child's return.

Sue seeks to live in expectation that her son Joel will rediscover faith: 'It isn't over until it's over! I will not give up hope. God is still in the business of doing miracles. I am going to seek to show Joel God's unconditional love, while praying fervently and with expectancy for his heart to change.'

After many years of faithful prayer Annette's husband Paul came to faith as a result of a dream. She writes, 'I have seen what the Lord has done in my husband. God can move mountains and I am asking him to reveal himself to Sophie, my daughter.'

Pray at all times and with all requests

Sally brought up three children as a lone parent and has since remarried. She writes: 'Prayer is essential. It is powerful and nothing will change without prayer. Keep on praying and ask others to pray too. Don't lose hope. God is faithful.'

Keep on praying and ask others to pray too

Prayer is the weapon God has given us to withstand the schemes of the enemy. As we pray, our most heartfelt cry to God will be for our children to return to him, but there are many other wonderful things that we can pray that can help them along the way. There is no set formula and we can pray God's blessing on every aspect of their lives. We can pray scripture over them. We can pray for Christian friends and people of influence to come into their lives. We can pray that God would use every opportunity to speak to them and that their eyes would be opened to see the things of God. We can pray on our own in the secret place, with our husband or wife or with friends. We can pray in the morning or the evening, for minutes or hours. We can pray in their room, while doing the washing up, on the phone, on the bus. We can find a special place where we can get away and pray for our children. We can take any and every opportunity to pray. I have prayed in all these situations and for all these things and more for our children. Some prayers have been answered and others not yet, but I continue to pray, trusting God's heart for them is even bigger than mine and reminding myself that they are his total obsession.

God's heart for them is even bigger than mine

Anna

A few months ago I met up with an old friend who arranged for me to meet Anna. Anna had been a grandmother figure to my friend's four children and had prayed for them every day through some turbulent teenage years. On the morning of my visit she was in pain from her hip, so was still in bed when I knocked on the door. She was lying back with the television on, wearing a bright red nightdress, her silver head resting on the pillow. Pictures of her children and grandchildren lined the walls of her small room. Her face lit up as I entered. She had suffered a stroke a couple of years ago and so had great difficulty communicating, but she refused to let that be an obstacle and motioned for me to sit down and talk with her.

She spoke falteringly, explaining that God would prompt her how to pray, often giving her special Bible verses. She beckoned me to come near. 'I am thankful to God for the stroke,' she whispered. 'I have more time to pray and to hear his voice.'

Anna knows her heavenly Father intimately and is in constant conversation with him for the children he has placed on her heart. She reminds me of another Anna living over two thousand years ago who 'never left the temple but worshipped night and day, fasting and praying' and who 'gave thanks to God and spoke about the child' (Luke 2:37, 38).

I asked her if she had any other insights to share. We sat in silence for several minutes and then her blue eyes lit up and a smile broke out across her lined faced. Although previously she had only been able to speak a few words at a time, the words of Psalm 23 seemed to flow from deep within:

'The LORD is my shepherd, I lack nothing. He makes me lie down in green pastures, he leads me beside quiet waters, he refreshes my soul. He guides me along the right paths for his name's sake. Even though I walk through the darkest valley, I will fear no evil, for you are with me; your rod and your staff, they comfort me. You prepare a table before me in the presence of my enemies. You anoint my head with oil; my cup overflows. Surely your goodness and love will follow me all the days of my life, and I will dwell in the house of the LORD for ever.'

'That's it,' she said. 'Goodness and love ... all their days.'

Reciting the psalm changed her; it was as if a dam had been breached and verse upon verse of scripture followed, stored up in her heart over many faithful years. One particular verse she repeated over and over again: 'I have made you and I will carry you, I have made you and I will carry you' (Isaiah 46:4).

I know I have to trust they are in his hands.

She reached out and held my hand: 'Don't take control,' she said. 'Just trust him. All the children are in God's hands.'

With an arthritic finger she pointed to a plant on the window sill: 'Plant seeds in their lives, water them with tears and prayers, give them the warmth of love, watch them grow.'

This woman of faith asked me for the names of my own children so she could pray for them. I wrote them down on a scrap of paper which she placed carefully by the bed. I know if I return to visit that paper will be worn and creased and will have been prayed over many times.

Praying for other parents' children is costly for Anna, and she knows all too well that there are no guarantees. As I stood up to leave she whispered to me, 'I pray for my own children too.' Anna has seen many children that she has prayed for come to faith, but not yet her own. 'I ask God why, and then I know I have to trust, trust they are in his hands.'

Chapter 6

Trees by the river

Jo Swinney

For Christians, the Bible is more than an ancient book; it is a revelation of God. It is one of the ways we hear him speak, it is an account of how and why and what he is doing in the world, and it is where we go to for guidance. If we are trees, the Bible is the river that nourishes our roots and makes sure our 'leaf does not wither' (Psalm 1:3). It is right, therefore, that we go to the Bible as a first port of call when we are in trouble. As we face the pain of seeing our children choose not to walk with God, the Bible is a vast reservoir where we can draw comfort, hope and wisdom for the way ahead.

Sometimes, in our panic, we might be tempted to yank out a phrase, a 'promise', holding on to it as a contractual guarantee to keep us sane during those 3.00am vigils. John White writes, 'Many parents get hurt because they find false hope in the Bible. I do not mean that the Bible is unreliable but that in their concern for their children, parents may read the Bible through magic spectacles.'[6] We may need to let go of false hope – such as any kind of guarantee that our children will become Christians – but there is plenty of true hope. Let's explore.

No blame, no credit

There is a pervasive belief that parenting follows this formula: good parenting = good, God-fearing children and bad parenting = bad, atheist children. This belief, whether or not we know we have it, is behind a good deal of anguish. Angela said to me, 'We berated ourselves and we compared ourselves to other families in the church whose children were all following God. We studied what they had done, trying to figure out where we'd gone wrong. We felt guilty and responsible. We felt we were failures.' But the Bible does not support this connection between good parents and good children and bad parents and bad children. If we were ever tempted to assume that God-fearing parents produce God-fearing offspring, reading the accounts of the kings of Judah will take that idea and put it through a mincer.

We felt guilty ... We felt we were failures

---

[6] John White, *Parents in Pain*, IVP, 1979, p41

Read through 2 Kings and you'll find that although the godly King Asa fathered another godly king, Jehoshaphat, there the line goes bad again. Jehoram 'did evil in the eyes of the LORD' (2 Kings 8:18). Jehoram's son Ahaziah followed in his father's footsteps, but his son, Joash 'did what was right in the eyes of the LORD' (2 Kings 12:2). He reigned for 40 years, during which time he repaired the Temple, and was eventually assassinated by his officials. So far, so random. His son Amaziah, who succeeded him to the throne, was strongly influenced by his father and did good in a limited kind of way: 'In everything he followed the example of his father Joash.

The Bible does not support this connection between good parents and good children

The high places, however, were not removed; the people continued to offer sacrifices and burn incense there' (2 Kings 14:3,4). Even Amaziah's death mirrored that of his father, and he was assassinated by his own people. His son Azariah (also known as Uzziah) was made king at the age of 16, and became a third generation of kings who pleased God (2 Kings 15:3), reigning for 52 years. Azariah's son Jotham also did right in the eyes of God (2 Kings 15:34), so perhaps my theory is flawed. Four generations of God-fearing kings – that's impressive. Must be a pattern. But

Jotham fathered a real rotter, a prince among rotters in fact. King Ahaz '… sacrificed his son in the fire, engaging in the detestable practices of the nations the LORD had driven out before the Israelites' (2 Kings 16:3). He sent the Temple gold and silver as a gift to the king of Assyria to entice him to attack Israel, and he had his priest build a pagan altar that sat next to the Temple altar, which he had thoroughly vandalised, and brazenly offered sacrifices on both. And yet – you can guess what's coming – his son Hezekiah 'did what was right in the eyes of the LORD' (2 Kings 18:3).

What can be even more confusing about this progression from God-pleasing to evil-doing kings and back again is that God had made a covenant with their forefather David, which seemingly encompassed his son and all subsequent generations: '… when your days are over and you rest with your ancestors, I will raise up your offspring to succeed you, your own flesh and blood, and I will establish his kingdom. He is the one who will build a house for my Name, and I will establish the throne of his kingdom for ever. I will be his father, and he shall be my son. When he does wrong, I will punish him with a rod wielded by men, with floggings inflicted by human hands. But my love will never be taken away from him … Your house and your kingdom shall endure for ever before me' (2 Samuel 7:12–16).

Just one generation later, and things had gone wrong: 'The LORD became angry with Solomon because his heart had turned away from the LORD, the God of Israel, who had appeared to him twice ... So the LORD said to Solomon, "Since this is your attitude and you have not kept my covenant and my decrees, which I commanded you, I will most certainly tear the kingdom away from you ..."' (1 Kings 11:9,11). Didn't God promise his father that the kingdom would always be in the family? By the time of Jesus' birth, Israel had not had a ruler from David's family for 200 years – what are we to make of that?

As a parent of someone who doesn't identify themselves as a Christian, we may understandably take great comfort from this verse: "'My Spirit, who is on you, will not depart from you, and my words that I have put in your mouth will always be on your lips, on the lips of your children and on the lips of their descendants – from this time on and for ever," says the LORD' (Isaiah 59:21). It sounds like a promise, doesn't it? It sounds like something we can hold God to. But was there an unbroken line of God-followers from Isaiah's time until now? No. So, must we then conclude that God is a promise-breaker? Can we trust anything he says? The key to all of this is in understanding how a covenant works.

The nature of covenants

Old Testament covenants were promises to which God bound himself, but they were always conditional on a response; they involved a relationship between two parties, and both needed to keep their end of the deal. Consider the parallel with the covenant of marriage. Two people commit to belong to each other, to be faithful until death parts them, but both need to keep the promises for the marriage to survive. It is no good one person saying, 'I'm keeping my promise and I'm staying married to you whatever you do,' if the other person is living on the other side of the world with someone else. That is not a marriage in any meaningful sense.

God's purposes require our participation; they require our children's participation. Ezekiel 18 spells out clearly each person's individual responsibility to respond to God: 'The one who sins is the one who will die. The child will not share the guilt of the parent, nor will the parent share the guilt of the child. The righteousness of the righteous will be credited to them, and the wickedness of the wicked will be charged against them' (v 20). So, yes, God has made a covenant of love with his people, and he will never fall through on his side, but he requires reciprocation. That is the deal.

God's purposes require our participation

But that is not the end of it. God can and does and has found a way to be faithful to us above and beyond his covenanted responsibilities. The New Testament is the account of a new covenant based on faith in Jesus Christ; all we need to do for our part in this one is believe.

Matthew's Gospel begins with a genealogy, Jesus' lineage traced back all the way to Abraham, who made the first covenant with God: 'I will make you into a great

We can trust him to do everything to win over our children, except ...

nation ... and all peoples on earth will be blessed through you' (Genesis 12:2,3). Between Abraham and Jesus there were some incredible hiccups, failures so profound that it is astonishing God kept going with his plan to save the world through this bloodline. Judah fathered a son by his daughter-in-law Tamar, Boaz was the son of a prostitute, David conceived a son with a woman who was married to someone else, even the dastardly Ahaz has his place as an ancestor of the Messiah. Jesus is the fulfilment of promises made over a period of two thousand years, during which time the human race did its best to derail the rescue mission over and over again. God's purposes are good and will be fulfilled, and we can trust him to do everything to win over our children, except force them against their own will.

Our Father

So our children are God's children. He has no grandchildren. When I became a mother I remember feeling I was just starting to catch a glimpse of what it meant that God loved me as a father. I knew what it meant to be loved, but I hadn't begun to understand the violence of emotion that a parent has towards their child, the absolute willingness to do *anything* to protect them, the enchantment with their features and their unfurling personality, the wholehearted commitment to their well-being. If we look at our children and feel those things, how much more does God? He loves our children. They are his children too. We want them to find salvation, to know peace with their maker; so does he. As it says in 1 Timothy, '... God our Saviour ... wants all people to be saved and to come to a knowledge of the truth' (2:3,4). When we have a child who doesn't want to know God, we share our pain with the creator of the universe. He is their father and he wants them close to his heart, not wandering around somewhere far away hurting themselves.

As their father, God has given them freedom. He wants them to choose to love him, and he is willing for them to make mistakes in their journey to that choice. As human parents, our inclination is to cut out as many opportunities for failure as possible, to do all we can to make sure our children do well – to control the outcome. God was OK with giving us all, from Adam and Eve onwards, genuine freedom, because he had dealt with every possible outcome – even the worst. Revelation 13:8 refers to '... the Lamb who was slain from the creation of the world.' The rescue plan was in place even before disaster struck. What God wants is not a child who obeys him because if they don't there'll be consequences, but one who loves him and wants to please him.

If God is OK with our children's freedom, we absolutely have to be OK with it too.[7]

Joelle and Tony have two daughters aged 21 and 19. Meredith, the eldest, was raped when she was 16. This precipitated a downward spiral as she lashed out against God and her church and became self-destructive in the process. She became promiscuous, stopped attending school and ran away on several occasions for days at a time. She fell in with a group of friends who Joelle describes as 'a bad crowd of disaffected teenagers', got into debt and began to steal from her family. When things got particularly bad, they asked her to leave home, feeling the need to put in boundaries to protect their younger daughter and themselves. She was gone for six months, and it was torture for the whole family.

In reflecting over the past few years, Joelle says, 'We haven't felt anger towards God. He never promised us that hard stuff wouldn't happen, but that he would be with us through it. There have been times when my interaction

---

[7] Danny Silk's book, *Loving our Kids on Purpose*, was the inspiration behind these two paragraphs.

with God was non-existent, when I was merely coping and getting through the day. However, he has shown me that

He knows what it is like to have rebellious, ungrateful and hurting children

he knows what it is like to have rebellious, ungrateful and hurting children, and his heart breaks for us. I found this very comforting and I have been learning to truly hand the girls over to him.'

She continues, 'I believe that God has his hand on both my girls – they have had encounters with him and they know in their hearts that he is there for them. My prayer is that they are both totally captivated by him and that they start to work out their own relationship with him. However, I love them as they are and accept it must be their decision.'

Being born to parents who know God may make us more likely to want to know him too, but it doesn't make us Christians by birthright. Each of us has to come to God ourselves. Danny Silk, in his excellent parenting book *Loving our Kids on Purpose*, writes this:

'We try to convey to our kids that we are in control of their lives from the time they are tiny … [The] problem with that lesson is that Heaven is not trying to control your life. God doesn't want to control you. Remember, in the presence of the Lord there is freedom, not control (2

Cor 3:17). We sing songs all day long about how God is in control. He does not control you, and neither does your wife, your boss, or your children. No one controls you. As a matter of fact, we've been given a Spirit of power, love and self-control (2 Tim 1:7 BBE). You cannot blame your life on God.'[8]

Jesus explained this to a man named Nicodemus, a member of the Jewish ruling council, who had his confidence in his lineage undermined when he was told to his great bafflement that 'no one can see the kingdom of God unless they are born again' (John 3:3). What Jesus was getting at was that being children of God means being born of the Spirit (3:6). It all comes down to whether or not each of us believes in the sacrifice made by the Son of Man for the sins of us all (3:18). Our belief doesn't automatically transfer via DNA to our offspring. They have to be born a second time to be part

The responsibility for getting our kids into the kingdom of heaven is not ours

of God's family. Why is this comforting? It is comforting because the responsibility for getting our kids into the kingdom of heaven is not ours. We are free to love our

---

[8] Danny Silk, *Loving our Kids on Purpose*, Destiny Image Publishers, 2008, p52

child, to love God and to drop the agenda. It is not on our shoulders.

The way of wisdom

One verse that has caused pain to parents is Proverbs 22 verse 6: 'Start children off on the way they should go, and even when they are old they will not turn from it.' As an observation of how things *generally* turn out, this is pretty accurate. Barna (USA) reports that, 'Most of the religious beliefs, behaviours and expectations that define a person's life have been developed and embraced by the age of 13.'[9] If this verse is taken as a promise, however, when our child does not continue in the way they should go, there are only two conclusions we can draw: either we didn't start them off in the right direction, or God is a liar. But this is not a promise, so don't worry, neither conclusion is warranted. The book of Proverbs belongs to the wisdom tradition, which consists of inspired reflections and observations on life by wise people. It draws attention to common patterns and the usual consequences of certain choices, for instance, 'All hard work brings a profit, but mere talk leads only to poverty' (14:23). Proverbs is a place we can look to for godly wisdom on raising our children, but it is not a prediction of the future.

---

[9] Quoted from *Faith Journeys* by Christian Research

The Bible isn't a parenting manual, but it is a manual for knowing and loving God. If we pursue God heart, mind and soul, and love our children in a way that reflects the way we have experienced the love of God, we have done all we can to usher them into the kingdom too. And even if we totally blow it in every way possible, God is on their case.

There is real cause for hope for our unbelieving children in the Bible. Psalm

The Bible isn't a parenting manual, but it is a manual for knowing and loving God

145 begins with praise: 'I will exalt you, my God the King … Every day I will praise you and extol your name for ever and ever' (vs 1,2). And this is something that we can choose to do, as David did. Because of our love for him, we will be compelled to pass on what we've experienced to our children: 'One generation commends your works to another; they tell of your mighty acts' (v 4). And the generations will each see for themselves the greatness of God, because his kingdom and his dominion are enduring and not limited to a certain period of history (vs 10–13). All anyone has to do to be saved is cry out to him. He is close and he will hear (vs 18,19).

The main source of our hope for our children's salvation, however, is in God's character. He is good (v 7), he is

95

righteous (vs 7,17), he is 'gracious and compassionate, slow to anger and rich in love' (v 8). He keeps promises (v 13), he is a generous provider (vs 15,16). We can trust that he will be as good to our children as they will allow him to be.

Chapter 7

Leaders' kids: a special case?

Katharine Hill

I imagine all of us have been tempted at times to put our leaders on a pedestal, and then to comment or judge when they have wobbled or, in some cases, got things wrong and fallen off altogether. Whether we are leaders or followers, my hope is that this chapter will help to bring some insight and understanding to the particular pressures that leaders and their families face.

The breakfast show this morning ran with the breaking news that a celebrity had been arrested on suspicion of a significant criminal offence. She is, of course, innocent until proven guilty, but in a matter of hours has become a prisoner in her own home. The paparazzi are encamped on the grass outside, hoping to get a glimpse of her silhouette against the window as she puts the kettle on, or to get a photograph as she attempts to leave the house to take her children to school. Reporters have been taken off other assignments in order to cover the case. This evening's papers will reveal her family history, past indiscretions will be rehearsed and columnists will speculate about her future. Her partner and her children will be included in the coverage. Privacy may be a common-law right, but it is one frequently disregarded when there is the opportunity to inform or, perhaps more accurately, entertain the public.

Forfeiting the right to privacy is the price paid for enjoying a celebrity lifestyle and, although the rewards of Christian leadership may be poles apart from this, they come with a similar price tag. As leaders, our decisions, our choices, our character – in fact all aspects of our lives, however personal – can come under the spotlight. We may expect this for ourselves, but what can take us by surprise is when the shaft of light widens to include our family and, in particular, our children.

When our children were young, many happy Saturday afternoons were spent at Bristol Zoo Gardens. On wet days, the first port of call would be Insect World. One of the favourite attractions was a large glass-fronted display of leafcutter ants living in a rain forest. The children would spend hours, small noses pressed against the glass, watching the ants go about their daily business. Industriously, the ants would cut leaves that were twice the size of their bodies and carry them on their backs, marching in line across the terrain to their chosen destination. They were oblivious to the fact that their everyday existence had become a spectator sport, and simply continued, business as usual, regardless of the crowd.

In the same way, the family life of leaders across all walks of life, but particularly those involved in church leadership, can become a spectator sport. Taking up the leadership challenge invariably involves the leader's entire family stepping onto the podium and becoming subject to public scrutiny and gaze. It is one thing for leaders themselves to accept this challenge, but it is quite another for their children to find themselves drawn into something that they didn't sign up to in the first place.

I remember the day as if it were yesterday. Hope triumphed over experience as I attempted to do the weekly shop with three tired and hungry children under 5 years' old. To make it worse, I was expecting child number four and was overcome by waves of nausea every few minutes. Children numbers two and three were strapped into the double supermarket trolley, with number one attempting to ride on the wheels. We survived the vegetable and fruit aisles and were making our way to the yoghurts when it happened. I turned my back for what can only have been a few seconds to reach a tin from the shelf, but it was more than enough time for our outrider to climb onto the side of the trolley and pull it, complete with fruit, veg and, more importantly, his brother and sister (who remained strapped in), on top of him. I am not sure if Tesco has heard a commotion like it before or since. There were three screaming children – one underneath the trolley and two dangling upside down – and fruit and veg rolling across the aisle. It was, to say the least, an eventful shopping trip.

The thing that has stayed indelibly etched in my mind is not the trolley crash itself, but the reaction of a bystander who recognised me from my leadership role at church. Picking up some stray oranges that were rolling towards her, she looked me in the eye and expressed her concern at my wayward offspring. Her exact words were, 'I would have thought someone like you would have better behaved children.' Ouch! I may have been at fault in embarking on the expedition in the first place, but it now appeared

I would have thought someone like you would have better behaved children!

that as a leader I was being held accountable for my son's decision to pull the trolley over. I realised at that moment that once you take on the mantle of leadership, in whatever capacity, higher standards are expected of you and you may be judged accordingly. Although, in this case, I did have some control over my children in the supermarket and probably could have handled things differently, as leaders there will be decisions our children make in the future over which we have no control.

There are three particular sources of pressure on leaders and their families:

Pressure from outside

First, we may feel that we are being judged by others. But is this pressure justified and what does the Bible have to say on the subject? As a parent in leadership, reading Paul's advice to Timothy (1 Timothy 3:4) has always caused me a degree of angst. He says that those who can't manage their own families well should not serve in church leadership. The specific role he refers to is that of an overseer, the term for a leader in a local congregation. Paul follows this with the instruction to Titus that when appointing elders he should see that that they are someone 'whose children believe and are not open to the charge of being wild and disobedient' (Titus 1:6). Scary? Yes. But before every church leader with teenagers begins writing a letter of resignation, it is vital that we first consider the historical context of the day.

When Paul wrote to Timothy in around AD 65, the role of the leader in the family was very different from today. The head of the household, or paterfamilias, was responsible for the entire household, including any children and slaves, and the role was taken very seriously. If anyone stepped out of line, the paterfamilias had absolute authority to deal with them. In serious cases this could include sending them into exile or even pronouncing the death penalty. There was no other system for dealing with errant behaviour (the court system existed only for full citizens), so the head of a household was the legal system for those under his responsibility. If a father in New Testament times failed in his role to 'manage' his household when children or slaves broke the law, it would have implications beyond the family, threatening the safety of others and the whole structure of society. It was obvious therefore that such a paterfamilias would not be a suitable leader for the church.

Taking the historical context into account, we can see that Paul's counsel needs to be applied very differently today. As leaders we would be wise to do everything in our power to bring up our children to follow Jesus, but we must do so in the knowledge that they may yet choose a different path. If the outcome is that our children choose not to follow Jesus, it does not then mean that as parents we are disqualified from church leadership.

The church ... couldn't have been more supportive

Graham writes about his experience as a church leader when his teenage daughter became pregnant: 'It was a traumatic time. I felt shame, anger and humiliation. I went to the leadership team and offered my resignation. I felt responsible for her actions and felt I couldn't continue in my role. The church, however, couldn't have been more supportive. They insisted I stay on and we felt totally held and supported by our church family.'

Wouldn't it be wonderful if all our churches responded in this gracious and loving way?

Paul doesn't, however, absolve us from all responsibility. Because, as leaders, we are role models, we do need to seek to set an example to our children. Our family needs to be our first priority; even if our children have left home and have children of their own, our actions and our attitudes can affect how easy it is for them to love God.

I spoke to Harvey, a student whose parents have been involved in different aspects of church leadership. Looking back on his days as a spirited member of the church youth group he gives a different perspective: 'My parents were just family, nothing special; we saw each other every

I do think that as a leader's child my behaviour reflected on them

day, so I felt it was unreasonable when there were times when I was expected to behave differently, just because of who they were. However, now I have left home I see things differently, and I do think that as a leader's child my behaviour reflected on them. I did have influence and the opportunity to set an example to others.'

Pressure from within

Rob Parsons[10] tells the story of the pastor and author Wayne Cordeiro who was asked to meet with a group of senior American church leaders. During the conference he asked them to name their greatest fear. One answer stood out among all the others: 'I just don't want my kids growing up hating God because of me.' I imagine this answer resonates

I just don't want my kids growing up hating God because of me

with leaders everywhere. We fear that the calling on our lives may make it harder for our children to love God, and when it seems that they have chosen a different path, we all too easily blame ourselves and our role.

As leaders, the greatest pressure can come from ourselves. We can set ourselves impossible standards and feel that our children's choices in some way reflect on our success and value as leaders. Alison writes: 'As a pastor, my husband has found it hard to accept our son's antagonism to spiritual things. He takes it personally that he was not able to convince his own son about faith.'

There are many burdens as a leader, but bearing total responsibility for whether our children are following Jesus,

[10] Rob Parsons, *Getting Your Kids Through Church Without Them Ending Up Hating God*, Monarch, 2011, p7

and feeling a failure as a leader if they aren't, isn't one of them.

Pressure on the children

A third kind of pressure comes into play: the pressure on the children themselves.

Gavin Calver's parents Ruth and Clive are well-known leaders in the evangelical world. He writes:

'Leaders' kids are not often allowed to be just young Christians with their own struggles; they have to be a certain type of Christian. They can often be expected to be 'the next whoever', and many older Christians try to encourage this.'

He goes on, 'A lot of people wanted me to be the next Clive Calver ... The pressure of it all was immense. It seemed as if everyone wanted me to be a little Clive, but I just wanted to be Gav. If I had been left alone to be a young Christian like the rest, then I would probably have coped better. However, if people were going to place too high an expectation on me then that was it. I'd just jack it all in.'[11]

If I had been left alone ... I would probably have coped better

---

[11] Gavin Calver, *Disappointed with Jesus?*, Monarch, 2004, p19

Aiden's parents were leaders in the church and he remembers clearly the feeling of being singled out and treated differently from his peers: 'Each summer our family would go to a Christian festival with a group from our church. I used to enjoy going, but if I'm honest the "God" part began to mean less and less over the years, but I would still enjoy going along to be with my friends. The last time I went, a few of us decided to miss the evening meeting and stayed in our tent drinking vodka that we had managed to buy in the local town in the afternoon. We all had far too much to drink, and were in a bad way the next day. What I felt was unfair was that I seemed to get into much more trouble than anyone else. I remember one of the other parents saying to me, "I would have expected you to set an example." The fact that my parents were leaders didn't have anything to do with me, but it meant that I was judged by a different standard than everyone else.'

Poppy, a church leader's daughter, writes of her experience: 'Unlike other parents' jobs it becomes a large part of your life, because you are literally seeing what living with faith is like (its ups and downs). I went along with it until I hit my teenage years, when I just found it irrelevant to my life at the time. Not only was my dad the local vicar in our village, but he was also the school chaplain at my girls' school. Although he was popular, there was no escape from it all.'

She continues, 'As a vicar's daughter I am so aware of all the politics and stuff that goes on and increasingly I watch my parents work so hard and long with little thanks. I'm full of admiration and fury at what they are doing to themselves.'

Richard Foster is an influential Christian writer and leader. His son Nathan Foster writes in his book *Wisdom Chaser*: 'As a child I was proud of my dad. Hearing him speak to crowds filled me with excitement. Perhaps he would mention my name or tell a story about me, or in some way acknowledge his home life. Somewhere along the way my feelings shifted to embarrassment and anger that dad had "holier" work to do. By thirteen I was filled with rage and shut down. When I was younger, people seemed to think that they knew something about my world because they had read one of Dad's books. Maybe they did know something, but because I hadn't given them the information it felt like a kind of violation.'[12]

Surviving and thriving

Growing up as a child of a Christian leader is not all bad; there can also be huge privileges.

Hannah writes, 'I was always aware of the effect that my brothers' choice to no longer continue with Jesus had had

---

[12] Nathan Foster, *Wisdom Chaser*, IVP, 2010

on my parents. Seeing how hard they found that was often what motivated me to staying involved in church, even when I wasn't sure I wanted to. Although I am so glad I did continue, it was undoubtedly hard, and meant it wasn't until I moved away to university that I really considered for myself what I wanted for my life. Even then the expectation to be the "great Christian child" of Christian leaders was evident for me. That pressure wasn't put upon me by my parents, but was more about what I thought was expected of me. I think it's fairly normal for children of families where Christ is so important to feel this pressure, and to some extent it is not a bad thing. It's just something where a balance needs to be found, so the child knows they are accepted despite the decisions they make.'

... the expectation to be the 'great Christian child' of Christian leaders was evident for me

One of the most important dates in my husband Richard's and my diaries is an evening with another couple who have become two of our closest friends. They are also both leaders and parents, and we meet together to eat, to laugh, to cry and to pray. For all of us it is an opportunity to 'say it like it really is', to share the joys and challenges of life, and to pray for each other. We have given each other permission to ask the tough questions. In challenging times, this couple has been a tower of strength for us, and I hope at times we have been able to be the same for them.

Many leaders can testify to the extraordinary pressure on family life when we put our heads above the parapet. Carrie wrote a handbook for parents on the issues surrounding sexual promiscuity in young people. On the day it was published her teenage daughter told her that she was pregnant. Richard and I can predict with remarkable accuracy the timing of disagreements between us – generally immediately before or after giving a marriage seminar.

The Bible encourages us to be self-controlled and alert because the enemy of our souls 'prowls around like a roaring lion' (1 Peter 5:8) and we are not to be unaware of his schemes. Becoming leaders does not mean that it is inevitable that there will be difficulty in our families, but it does seem to increase the number of arrows coming in our direction. What better way to disarm a leader and render them ineffective than to cause division and discouragement in their home? But we can 'be strong in the Lord and in his mighty power.' We can 'put on the full armour of God, so that [we] can take [our] stand against the devil's schemes.' We can 'take up the shield of faith, with which [we] can extinguish all the flaming arrows of the evil one' (Ephesians 6:10,11,16).

This is not barcode Christianity. Irrespective of our

position in leadership, our children will make their own decisions in life and we cannot guarantee the outcome. What we can do is pursue God for ourselves and seek to make our homes, our churches and the places where we have influence as leaders places of grace, welcome and forgiveness where it is easy to belong.

Chapter 8

Lifestyle choices

Jo Swinney

What we believe inevitably works its way out in how we behave, and if our children do not share our Christian convictions, the chances that they are going to sign up to a Christian code of behaviour are slim to none. This is not to say that Christians have a monopoly on good character or standards of morality or a sense of social responsibility – we all know that isn't the case. But in today's society, the Christian way is not the norm, most particularly when it comes to sexual behaviour, but also around other issues such as alcohol and finances. From the teen years onwards, lifestyle issues can be a major area of tension within families, and they are often the fulcrum of the conflict around religious belief.

The way we handle the lifestyle choices of our children depends upon the answers to three questions:

- Are they under 18, and/or living in our home?

- Do they profess to be Christians?
- Is what they are doing illegal or dangerous to themselves or others?

We will look later on in this chapter at what can be done if the answer to any of these is 'yes'. But we also need to think about what to do when the answer to all the questions is 'no', because that is a densely populated place to stand. There are multitudes of parents uneasily shuffling around on this rough terrain, not sure where to put their feet but knowing this is not where they want to be. And if this is us, I don't think we need to be there.

Life, oh life!

Why is it so very painful when our children make choices that fly in the face of biblical teaching? There are points along the way that people commonly cite as particularly hard – when a son or daughter first refuses to go to church, when they begin to show scepticism about the way the Christian worldview answers the big questions of human origins or suffering, when they excuse themselves from family prayer times and stop reading the Bible. But by far the most difficult thing for many parents is when their teenager becomes sexually active. In secular western society this is a morally neutral rite of passage, but for a Christian sex is an act that God designed to unite two people together for life.

Holly says, 'I live with my current boyfriend and this

is something that is surrounded by a bit of an awkward silence. I can tell my parents are upset about it. At first I played it down, telling them that I was just there until I found my own place, but then I stayed on. I don't know if they have got used to the idea yet.'

For years, Kylie felt horrible guilt knowing the way she was living didn't match up to the biblical standards she had had drummed into her while growing up. But she says, 'Eventually, with maturity, I started to rationalise things. Why would I go to hell for sleeping with a man I love just because I'm not married to him? By questioning things instead of accepting them I managed to work out that I'm not a bad person; I'm a normal person.'

Alfie says, 'The worst time in my relationship with my parents was when I said I was moving in with my girlfriend. I rang my parents to tell them and to discuss it, out of respect. They jumped in the car and drove two hours to see me. They were both in tears, pleading with me not to do it. It was a horrible time. I did move in with her, and it was great to have

We were made to feel as though we had caused everyone great pain

someone to love me for me. But my parents took out their disappointment on her, and didn't welcome her into the family. We were made to feel as though we had caused everyone great pain. We didn't deserve to feel like that, and my girlfriend especially didn't – she had been nothing but nice. It caused a big rift between us and the rest of the family.'

I think there are several reasons why a person moving in with their partner can bring tensions in a family to a head. First, it is a very open and public declaration that they are choosing to divert from the ways in which they have been brought up. Parents who may have been able to gloss over their child's waning enthusiasm for church among their Christian friends are forced to come clean about the true state of things when it involves permanent living arrangements. Pride can be wounded. No one wants to admit that they mind how things look, but we all do to some degree, if we are honest.

We need to respect their decision, whether or not we agree with it

Second, it has the effect of deflating hope. It seems final, an official declaration that, for them, God is dead. There may have been no evidence of a spiritual ember for years, but for some reason, a decision to cohabit has the ring of a death knell.

Third, there is the sheer disappointment of seeing them make a decision that we believe deep down is not God's best for them. We want the best for our children. We long for them to be happy. And a big part of that happiness is found within the relationships they have along the way. Many parents begin praying for their child's future spouse when they are still cooing on the changing mat – I know I did. Although it is now pretty standard for people to live together outside of wedlock, there is evidence to suggest that this form of relationship is less stable. We genuinely fear that it will blow up in their face.

All these reasons are totally understandable, but they can, as they did in Alfie's family, lead to a breakdown in relationship. The fact is, if our child is an adult, if they are living independently from us, if they are not a disciple of Christ and if their behaviour is not illegal or dangerous, then we need to respect their decision, whether or not we agree with it. A Christian lifestyle is the outworking of the Spirit within a person. Holiness is a lifelong journey for all of us, and we can be in danger of getting sexual sin out of all proportion. Yes, it may be hard for us to see our children become sexually active before marriage, but the greater issue is that they don't know and love God,

We can be in danger of getting sexual sin out of all proportion

and so don't desire to make choices that will please him.

And we could be so blinded by the enormity of the sexual stuff going on where it shouldn't be that we miss all the good things that are going on: the stirrings of compassion for the poor or righteous anger at injustice; a spiritual hunger that is leading them to pray even as they are unsure whom they are addressing; a sense that they can't shake off that they are part of a bigger story. I don't mean to imply that how we behave sexually is irrelevant. It matters to us and it matters to God. But bring to mind the sexual record of some of the biblical characters beloved of God and you have to admit it doesn't seem

His grace goes on and on ... and so should ours

to be a deal breaker. Abraham slept with his wife's servant Hagar – at his wife's suggestion. David committed adultery. Solomon had 700 wives and 300 concubines (Hugh Hefner eat your heart out).

Our children are more likely to be drawn to God if we behave towards them as he does, as he has towards his rebellious people throughout the ages – with unfailing love, mercy, grace, persistence and kindness. The grace on offer from God is not withdrawn on the day they sign a joint lease with their boyfriend or on the night they lose their virginity to a stranger in a toilet cubicle at a club. His grace goes on and on, hunting down the lost and the broken and the distant and the angry, and so should ours.

Bill and Louisa have two adopted children, Natalie and Benj, both of whom joined the family as babies. When they were children they engaged in their parents' faith and loved being a part of the church. Every morning they would have family prayers after breakfast, which was a fun time and one that the whole family enjoyed. Louisa explains what happened as they grew older:

'Benj drifted away – more of a lifestyle choice, but Natalie is more academic and made a decision not to continue with her faith. We haven't had the conversation as to what was at the root of them drifting away – they might tell us one day.

'They are both respectful of our position and very supportive of us. When both of them wanted to move in with their partners they came and asked if we could cope with it and said if we couldn't they wouldn't do it. We decided we couldn't force our children to live a lie. We wanted to accept them and their partners for who they are. We said we couldn't give them our blessing – we'd reserve that for marriage – but we would love them unconditionally.

God loved us when we were still sinners

'We have seen so many parents fall out with their children over lifestyle choices, in effect saying, "We will love you only if you are good and conform to what we would like you to do." God loved us when we were still sinners, so we wanted to reflect that in the way we loved our children.

'It is hard sometimes to see other families where children

are engaged with their parents' faith, but God has spared us the risk of being proud and thinking it is anything to do with us. We feel pain over them, and we agonise for them in prayer, but our relationship with both of them is strong, and we are grateful for that.'

Special circumstances

Under 18/living at home

Lifestyle issues may not be under our jurisdiction when it comes to independent, adult children, but they are when that person is under 18 and/or lives in our home. During the teen years, our influence as parents lessens, but it is still appropriate to maintain boundaries and guidelines. Of course, the goal is to enable our children to move into the world capable of making good and responsible choices, rather than to control them while we can, but there are plenty of tools to help in that regard, from positive reinforcement to repercussions for disobedience such as curfews or a freeze on the allowance. My friend Anna spent her teens at home playing Scrabble with her parents and occasionally going to the pub for a diet cola with her friends. She is unusual (Lord, grant me unusual teens like Anna!). A more average teenager will explore what the world has to offer and do a bit of damage along the way. As parents, wise advice is probably to pick our battles carefully – don't send in the artillery for an extra piercing; stick to our guns over the issues worth fighting over and hold on for dear life to the connection we have with them.

For older children who live at home there is a case to be made for honouring a house code of conduct, particularly if there are younger children around. Heidi and Ralph have recently allowed their 20-year-old daughter Samantha to move back home, but she has a history of destructive behaviour and they have set some specific conditions on her return: she must not steal, she must keep her room in a reasonable state, she has to contribute rent and either be at college or working. Heidi writes, 'We were very concerned that she would revert to previous behaviour, but apart from a few hiccups she is now doing better and it is lovely to see her blossoming into a more honest, disciplined young woman. One thing that became evident while she was away was how hard everything had been on our younger daughter. While she was gone we started to establish a more fun and deeper relationship with Evelyn. This is precious to us, and we won't allow it to be disrupted.'

Professing Christians

Sometimes our child may claim to be a Christian but be living a life that seems to undermine the truth of the claim. Barbara says of her daughter Ellen, 'She says she serves God, but she makes choices that don't line up with God's will for her life.' Brian writes, 'Our son Stuart made a commitment and attended church until the age of 16. He chose the path of the prodigal when he went away to university. While he would say he has a belief he does not follow that through with living it out.' Patricia says of her daughter Sarah, 'She began to drift away in her late teens. If asked, she would say she still believes in God, but she doesn't appear to have a personal ongoing walk with him.'

She says she serves God, but she makes choices that don't line up

True faith doesn't exist on a theoretical level – it is translated into reality or it is no faith at all: 'Those who belong to Christ Jesus have crucified the flesh with its passions and desires' (Galatians 5:24). And there is biblical imperative for holding fellow Christians to account, for example, '… if one of you should wander from the truth and someone should bring that person back, remember this: whoever turns a sinner from the error of their way will save them from death and cover over a multitude of sins' (James 5:19,20). The letter of James also reminds us that as well as sexual morality, our Father is concerned that we meet the needs of the poor, control our tongues, refuse to be selfishly ambitious or envious and so on – while remembering that the Lord is 'full of compassion and mercy' (5:11). So if our children are professing faith, it isn't inappropriate to challenge them about behaviour that contradicts their creed.

However, this is a very fine line to walk. Good behaviour is the fruit of knowing God, and much more important than addressing how they are living is praying for and encouraging our children towards a relationship with him.

Dangerous or illegal

From the age of 15, Ella's son Zac was sexually promiscuous, drank heavily, smoked and used drugs. Ella says, 'As a mother, you spend years giving them the right nutrition, teaching them to cross the road and looking after them physically. It's heartbreaking to see them wrecking themselves.' One of the elements of self-destructive behaviour that is so hard for parents to witness is that the child we have cherished and have poured our life into caring for is being mistreated. Although from a teenager's perspective it may seem stuffy and out of date, from a parent's point of view, reactions to harmful behaviour usually stem from love and protectiveness.

Sam's parents managed to convey this clearly to him. During his first year at university he drank extremely heavily, passing out several nights a week. He told his parents the gist of what was going on, and they came to visit him in Durham a few times. He remembers, 'They'd say things like, "This is bad for you. You're damaging your body." And they cut off my allowance, because they didn't want to fund my drinking. They gave me space to work out the spiritual thing, but they were very concerned about the alcohol, and that was because of what it was doing to me.'

If our child's behaviour is harming them, then it is almost impossible not to try and intervene. We are dealing with a primal parental instinct. But even in this situation, there is a limit to what we can do to protect our child from their own behaviour, and sometimes allowing them to experience the consequences of their choices is the loving thing to do.

When it comes to illegal behaviour – drug dealing, theft, assault and so on – we have a certain duty to the law (Romans 13:1–7). As agonising as it may be, as a responsible citizen we really need to be on the side of the police and cooperate with them as far as is fair and reasonable. Obviously this is a huge and complicated subject and, if it is one you are currently dealing with, I can highly recommend John White's book *Parents in Pain*, particularly the chapter called 'In Trouble with the Law'.[13]

The horse before the cart

As parents we can feel hurt, disappointed, fearful and angry when our children do things that run counter to God's ideal for them, and the way we raised them. But it is every adult's

---

[13] John White, *Parents in Pain*, IVP, 1979

prerogative to make their own decisions about how they live their lives. What we want from our children is not good behaviour, crafted to gain our approval, but a deep, inner understanding of who they are in Christ. Until they have that, of course they are not going to sign up for what they perceive as an empty code of behaviour: why would they?

Chapter 9

Staying connected

Katharine Hill

Sian heard the front door bang shut and then the familiar clatter as her son tripped over the pile of footwear in the hallway. The bedside alarm clock said 2.45am. She sighed and turned over, reflecting that her relationship with Ben was not what it used to be. Since they had moved house he had distanced himself from church and got involved with a new group of friends. Captivated by their company and the acceptance and freedom that this new lifestyle seemed to offer, he had begun to spend all of his free time away from home, often returning in the small hours of the morning. She was worried about his drinking too. She wasn't sure where he was getting the money from, but most nights he seemed to return home the worse for wear.

Anxious thoughts and concerns, the kind that become our bedfellows at night, began to press in. She glanced again at the clock: 4.20am. Sleep escaped her and she decided to get up and make a cup of tea. As she made her way to the kitchen she noticed that the bathroom light was on and the door was ajar. She was overwhelmed by the unmistakable stench of vomit. Ben was slumped behind the bathroom door, comatose. A heady cocktail of tenderness, rage, disappointment and exasperation overtook her. The strength of her emotions took her by surprise. She sat up with him for the rest of the night, a battle raging inside her: anger and exasperation at his behaviour fighting against an overwhelming sense of love and compassion for her son.

... anger and exasperation at his behaviour fighting against an overwhelming sense of love

It was CS Lewis who said, 'Love anything and your heart will be wrung and possibly broken. If you want to make sure of keeping it intact you must give it to no one, not even an animal.'[14]

As parents, many of us have found our hearts caught up in the tug of war between anger and pain and love and compassion, watching helplessly as our children make deliberate choices or slide into decisions that we fear may

---

[14] CS Lewis, *The Four Loves,* Harper Collins (reissue), 2002

have life-changing consequences. The problem is generally not that we don't love our children enough – it is that our love for them is overwhelming.

The challenge for most of us is how we demonstrate unconditional love for our children, even when the decisions they make disappoint us, so that they know that they are loved *anyway*.

When our children were very young, I would creep into their bedrooms at night and pray over them. Little hands that a few hours earlier had been covered in finger paints, faces that had been red with rage, feet that had been drumming the floor, now lay perfectly still and utterly peaceful. Often I would simply stand there and feel overwhelmed by the strength of my love for them. I would want time to stand still, to be able to capture the breathtaking beauty and simplicity of a child peacefully asleep. I would pray that they would have soft hearts that would respond to the love of their Father in heaven. As I prayed I would find it difficult to imagine a time when I would not be able to be the channel of God's amazing love for them.

Even though they are now young adults and three are away from home, I still often go into my children's bedrooms and pray for them. I still pray they would have hearts that are receptive to the love of the Father.

As for any family, the intervening years have brought joys and challenges. We are not living in a dream world and the passing of time has taught me some lessons along the way. I know that at times my reaction to my children's behaviour, whether fuelled by fear, disappointment, guilt or control, has not always modelled to them what the unconditional love of the Father looks like.

Paul, in writing to the Christians at Corinth, describes what that love is: 'Love is patient, love is kind. It does not envy, it does not boast, it is not proud. It does not dishonour others, it is not self-seeking, it is not easily angered, it keeps no record of wrongs. Love does not delight in evil but rejoices with the truth. It always protects, always trusts, always hopes, always perseveres. Love never fails' (1 Corinthians 13:4–8).

When we mess up in our parenting, as in every other situation in life, we can run to the arms of our heavenly Father who is always patient and kind, is not easily angered and who keeps no record of wrongs. We can trust him to give us all we need as we seek to show that same love to our children, whatever path in life they choose to take.

I remember once being at sea in a small boat; one minute we were in brilliant sunshine with clear skies ahead and the next in the centre of an incredible storm. In life, as in sailing, disasters can come out of a clear blue sky, and if our children decide not to follow the journey of faith we can feel as if the storm clouds have suddenly descended and we are unable to see the way ahead. In those times we need to be on the lookout for a lighthouse or other landmarks along the way to help keep us on course.

Every parent's journey is unique, but most will encounter both calm seas and choppy waters at different times along the way. As we have no control over the weather, neither do we control what circumstances come our way. But we do have some control over our response to those circumstances – and, in particular, our response to

Every parent's journey is unique

the child who may be at the centre of the storm. Over the 24 years that Richard and I have been parents there have been many challenging moments when we have longed for someone to give us a neat answer – to hand us a 'Survival Guide to Successful Parenting' with simple instructions on how to do the job well. But we have learnt that there are no quick fixes and that to ask 'how to' is the wrong approach. 'How to' focuses on outcomes and success; the approach we need to take leaves the outcome open. It looks at our character. It does not present us with an easy-to-follow flow chart, but offers an ongoing journey of relationship with our Father that will, in turn, influence the way that we parent our children.

As we seek to pass on that unconditional love to our children, what are the landmarks that will keep us on course?

Acceptance

Whatever decisions our children make in life, they (like us) have a deep need for acceptance.

Rob Parsons writes: 'What is the great longing of our heart? I have no doubt it is the endeavour to prove we are worth loving. For many of us, this compulsion is all consuming. Life screams at us: "You must be clever to be loved"; "You must be beautiful to be loved"; "You must be wealthy to be loved".

... our heart doubts that we are worthy of love

But life can have no idea how cruel it is to scream such things. Does it not know that already our heart doubts that we are worthy of love?'[15]

Our children have grown up in a world that tells them they need to earn acceptance, but as parents we have the opportunity to tell them a different story. We can tell them that they are accepted for who they are, irrespective of academic achievement, good looks, sporting prowess, leadership qualities or engagement with the things of God.

This is not to say there is no need for boundaries. Ella looked back on some difficult years with her son Zac: 'We were clear with him that if we found anything illegal in the house we would report him to the police. At the same

---

[15] Rob Parsons, *Getting Your Kids Through Church Without Them Ending Up Hating God*, Monarch, 2011, p109

time we worked hard to maintain the relationship. It was tough love. Paul, my husband, showed such strength, such patience and such love as a father. He gave clear boundaries but always left the way open for him to come back.'

Showing unconditional love to our children may also include showing love and acceptance to their friends, even if, in our honest moments, we find ourselves disappointed with the partners or friendship group they have chosen.

Nat and Helena commented about their relationship with their daughter Rosie: 'We did all we could to accept the various boyfriends that came and went. We refused to judge, although I'm sure she knew we didn't like her lifestyle. We regularly told her that we were proud of her, and indeed we were in many, many ways.'

Matt remembers the day he brought his girlfriend Lillie home to a family party. 'Most of the people invited were involved with church. Lil was in a group chatting, and she heard one of Mum's friends ask her if it was a big deal to her that my girlfriend wasn't a Christian. I hadn't mentioned anything to Lil

I'm sure she knew we didn't like her lifestyle

about Christianity, and the comment made her feel like it was club that she couldn't belong to. I think Mum and Dad tried to include her, but after that she always felt like an outsider, and a few months later we split up.'

Respect

A decision not to continue in the faith we have been taught is never taken lightly.

As parents, while continuing to pray for them, we can show our children at least that we respect their integrity in coming to this conclusion.

Lara writes: 'I think Mum and Dad are ashamed that neither of their children goes to church. My mum has made me feel like I'm a bad person because I don't follow religion and don't bring my kids up on it. But I try to teach them right from wrong and to be good people, and so far they've turned out OK and done well. I'd like Mum and Dad to respect me for that.'

Ella spent some focused time praying that her prodigal son, Zac, would return home. Her other son, Harry, was about to go travelling on his gap year, and she prayed that during that time his faith would deepen. In fact, while he was away, the reverse happened and he returned with the conviction that he no longer wanted to follow God. Describing her feelings she said: 'I couldn't believe it; the exact opposite of what I had been asking God for had happened. But as I thought about it I realised that what God had really done was to show me Harry's heart. There was no pretending. I worked hard to honour and respect his decision, but I felt real grief.'

Several years later God wonderfully answered her first

prayer and both her boys are now young men of faith.

Helena writes: 'When our second daughter moved in with her boyfriend I found it very difficult, and I know my attitude caused a distance to come between us. I apologised to her partner (after several years) and asked if we could begin again. Although our beliefs are very different, we have grown to accept and respect this young man.'

Simon and Cathy write: 'Perhaps one benefit of our early emphasis on honesty about questions meant that Tim was able to tell us how he felt and didn't continue to pretend faith – which in some ways we might have found easier! As a couple, we have stayed pretty much of one mind. Although we are sad that Tim does not share our faith at this time, we take care not to assume he will expect to be excluded from anything "Christian". Everything is out in the open, which is where we believe it should be. He respects our position and we respect his. It is unlikely that his views will change if he feels our regard for him is diminished by his position. We commend him to God and accept that everyone's journey is different. The Gospels seem to teach that Jesus had more regard for honest doubt than dishonest faith, and we want to respect that.'

No favouritism

The Bible is full of stories of parents who showed favouritism to one of their children. Rebekah, Jacob and

Jesse all found this a challenge. If we have more than one child and find that one is swinging from the chandeliers in the worship service and the other refuses to set foot in church, it can be difficult to demonstrate that we love both of them equally without favouritism.

Jane comments, 'We always try to treat the girls equally, but Tracey says she feels judged. I think at times she might have felt unloved.'

Harriet writes: 'I have a much closer relationship with Caroline as she has maintained her faith throughout, and so we see things from the same perspective. My other daughter, Bella, and stepdaughter, Emma, want nothing to do with church, and often gang up against her. When they do, I find that I too quickly jump to her defence. That makes relationships difficult and we have become guarded in what we say.'

The child who finds ... that faith is not for them will already know our disappointment

The truth is that the child who finds with all integrity that faith is not for them will already know our disappointment with their decision and can feel that the die is loaded from the outset.

We may well, at one level, have more in common with children who share our faith, but we need to work hard to show the others that this makes no difference to how much we love them.

Affirmation

One of the most helpful pieces of parenting advice Richard and I received over the years was to 'catch your children doing something right'. When boundaries have been tested I have found it so easy to slip into a downward spiral of criticism and negativity. But we have a powerful tool at our disposal if we can

Catch your children doing something right!

learn to spot the things that are going well and affirm our children for it.

Mercia writes: 'Our son has drifted away from church, but he is one of the kindest, most generous people I know. He will put himself out for anyone. I realise, looking back, that I had become so focused on the fact that his faith seemed to be dwindling that I stopped noticing the many other wonderful qualities he has.'

Showing love to our children, whatever age and whatever stage they are at, can mean choosing to find something positive about them and to praise them for it. More powerful still is to speak well of them to others in their presence. We have tried to make a point over the years of using significant birthdays or other special occasions as an excuse to gather friends together and to speak words of encouragement and affirmation about our children. Whatever distance there is between us, we can seek to speak, write, text, tweet or Facebook words of affirmation to our children whatever their situation and whatever life choices they have made. Proverbs 18:21 says, 'The tongue has the power of life and death.' We can speak words of life and blessing over our children's lives and demonstrate to them in a powerful way that we love them.

Loving against the odds

Annette's daughter, Sophie, became a Christian while at school, and through her Annette herself came to faith. While at university, Sophie met and fell in love with an engineer who was from another faith. She decided to convert. Annette writes: 'When she came home to tell us, our whole world fell apart. We begged her to reconsider. She said that she was going to leave university and marry him whether or not we agreed, and she did just that and moved abroad. For two years I tried to keep the lines of communication open, but it was very hard. I was gripped with fear for her safety. I felt anger, hurt and rejection; I felt I had been deceived and was overwhelmed with guilt. Time and again I asked myself where I had gone wrong as a mother that she would do this.'

During this time Annette's husband, Paul, experienced the

love of the Father in a powerful way and came to faith. The very next day he sent an email to Sophie. 'We hadn't spoken for three years and within minutes of receiving it she was on the phone. We booked flights and were reunited. They now have children of their own and are back in the UK. I find it so hard because she dresses differently because of her faith, and when the girls are older they will too. When she comes to visit us we can't invite anyone around. But I know that God has told me just to love her.'

Whatever decisions our children have made, however challenging the circumstances, we can look through God's lens of unconditional love and seek to make it the hallmark of our family life. As parents we can look to reflect the kind of relationship that God designed us to have with him; we can seek to be the parents to our children that God is to us. But we can do this only when we ourselves plumb the heights and depths of the unfathomable love that he has for us.

Chapter 10

The long view

Jo Swinney

I was born to Christian parents, who had been praying for me before I was even born. My dad was ordained and did his curacy in a thriving church in the north west of England. Some of my earliest and happiest memories are to do with that church, and I vividly remember praying a formal prayer to make sure I was officially signed up for heaven when I was about 4 years' old. It would be nice to be able to say that from that point on, like Samuel, I grew not only in stature but in favour with the Lord and with people (1 Samuel 2:26). It would be nice, but if I said it, I would be lying.

Here is an incomplete list of things I have changed my mind about over the years: mushrooms, England, leggings, the Labour party, dishwashers, mobile phones, cats, the colour brown, whether it is possible to enjoy exercise, euthanasia… Maybe I am particularly fickle, but I like to think that I am like everyone else, just in flux. My opinions adjust according to new information that comes my way, or experiences I have, or because my reasons for having taken the position start to look less compelling. And like everyone, my spiritual journey has not been entirely straightforward.

When I was 5, my family and I moved to the Algarve, where my parents founded a Christian environmental charity called A Rocha. I went to an international school and I didn't do very well socially, which is a gentle way of saying that I was an outcast, a loser, a drop-out, a pariah... It was really hard, and it didn't improve much during the eight years I was there. Initially my faith was very strong, and it probably didn't aid me in my quest for friends because I was of the hellfire and damnation persuasion. I took all my troubles to God, though, and prayed hard through lonely lunchtimes, muttering memorised scripture to myself ('Dear friends, do not be surprised at the fiery ordeal that has come on you to test you, as though something strange were happening ...' (1 Peter 4:12)). I was aware, too, of the ways God had provided for my family, of how the story of A Rocha was unfolding against the odds, and I knew my parents' faith was absolutely everything to them.

... I knew my parents' faith was absolutely everything to them

But at the tender age of 10, I grew a bit cynical. Christianity seemed dusty and removed, and I began to wonder if it was really my thing after all. It had caused me nothing but trouble as I saw it. I found the spiritual times we had as a family awkward and uncomfortable, and I began to detach. I am not sure how or if I communicated any of this to my parents, or if they knew, what they felt about it. It was a long time ago!

The next thing that happened could not have been engineered by anyone. We had some students come to stay on their way to Lisbon, and I went to the beach with them one afternoon. One of them prayed for me, and afterwards I was left in no doubt at all

I was left in no doubt at all that I had met with God

that I had met with God – and that not only was God real, he was interested in me personally. I imagine my mum and dad were pleased to see my passion for God reignited, but I must have been insufferable at the same time! This was my ultra-religious phase, and everyone knew about it.

Again, if you were my parents, you might have thought you could let out a deep breath and give thanks that one of your children had found their way. But they couldn't relax just yet. My teens were spent at boarding school and culminated in a gap year in Zimbabwe, pretending I didn't know God. When I told my boyfriend after several months rampaging drunkenly around southern Africa that I was, or had been, a Christian, his eyes popped out on stalks. According to him I was the antithesis of a Christian, which from his perspective was a compliment, but nevertheless gave me pause for thought.

... they weren't fazed ... when I experimented with life without God

From then on, we began huge religious debates which had the effect of me turning back to God and alienating him. Our relationship ended because we couldn't reconcile the directions we were taking. When I began university, I did everything I could to resurrect my dehydrated spiritual life. Although it hasn't been an uninterrupted trajectory towards godly maturity, since then the general direction has been towards Jesus.

My parents would hate to be set up as any kind of paragons for anyone else to follow, and I know they don't take credit for the way that their four children have forged relationships with God. But there are some things I am grateful for, that they happened to get right. They lived their own relationship with God very transparently, and it quite obviously informed their priorities, their thinking and their choices. They never made an issue of church attendance; in fact, my dad seemed to have many of the same struggles with church that we did, which we found hilarious. My mum was amazing at praying with and for us, writing us cards with apt Bible verses and giving us God-inspired advice about our concerns and anxieties. My dad was always good for a gnarly theological tussle. I often took him the arguments against God that my classmates had thrown at me, confident that he would be able to find a way for me to hold on to both my faith and my self-respect. And they weren't fazed — at least not that I knew about — when I experimented with life without God. Perhaps that is because I was on a different continent and hadn't given them the full picture of what I was up to, but I do think they also gave me some deliberate space to sort things out myself.

It's a long way to Tipperary

I have told you my story to illustrate the point that for many, perhaps even the majority of people, conversion is a lifelong process. Most of us have long and eventful journeys of spiritual discovery that see us speeding up the motorway in the wrong direction, stuck in lay-bys with empty petrol tanks, puttering up country lanes, kind of getting there but not very fast and dealing with all sorts of hazards along the way. If your daughter

> **Most of us have long and eventful journeys of spiritual discovery**

says to you, 'I don't believe in God and I am in no shape or form a Christian,' she is telling you how things are in that moment, but it does not mean that she has signed a contract keeping her fixed to that statement for the rest of her life. To assume that she has means you are liable to overreact.

Matt is a youth worker, used to having parents come to him in a flap about where their children are headed spiritually and wanting him to do something to turn them around. He says, 'I try to tell them not to be so stressed over it – their kids, as with us all, are on a long and complex journey, and not necessarily as far from God as they think.'

The fact is, few have shut the door fully on Jesus, even if it is locked and barred on church.

John says, 'I'm not sure when exactly I chose to walk away. I found I couldn't openly tell my parents what I had decided because it was just too painful. I wasn't rejecting my parents, or even really their faith, which I have great respect for. I have seen the fruit of their belief in God.

I wasn't rejecting my parents, or even really their faith

And I didn't want them to think it was the end of the process, and be more dramatic about it than they needed to be. I am still attuned to the spiritual side of life.'

At the age of 13 Gavin Calver was banned from the

church youth group for behaving badly, and from that time on he grew more and more disaffected with his parents' religion. And yet, after years of rebellion, things changed. As an adult, he wrote a book called *Disappointed with Jesus?*. He says, 'I actually remember buying my dad a book about cricket and writing inside the front cover, telling him about my surrender to Christ. It was too embarrassing to tell them, especially as I had lived with the strong conviction that I was right and hadn't wanted to back down. Things

A huge wall of tension was suddenly broken down and we were able to talk

were so different after giving my life to Jesus – it was a huge deal telling my folks. It totally changed my relationship with them, particularly because a huge wall of tension was suddenly broken down and we were able to talk in a way that we hadn't before.'

I am a terribly impatient person. It is hard for me to wait for things, and even short waits like the three minutes it takes to defrost my lunch in the microwave make me itchy with frustration. God's sense of timing is entirely different. His plans span centuries. He left the Israelites in slavery in Egypt for 400 years before leading them back to the Promised Land (Genesis 15:13–16). Hundreds more years passed between the first veiled prophecies about a coming

Messiah and the birth of Jesus. Jesus told his disciples to be ready for his imminent return in glory; two thousand years later we are still waiting.

We don't know for sure that our children will find God, but we can be sure that the fact it hasn't happened yet doesn't mean it won't.

Who sleeps on a bed of roses?

It could well be that some time down the line our child will have a story to tell worthy of a Christian paperback. We should never give up hope that they will find their way into God's embrace.

But the question remains, how can we live the intervening time well, in a way that enables our relationships with our child and with God to flourish?

When things don't happen as we hope they will, one of our reactions is often surprise and even shock. Somehow we think that if we parent our children in a certain way, if we honour God and pray for them and plug them into a decent church and love them, they will emerge into independent adulthood as committed Christians. When it doesn't happen we wonder which part of the formula we got wrong. Biblical Christianity doesn't promise a trouble-free life. We don't devote our lives to God on the premise that in return he'll iron out the bumps in the road for us. We love and serve God because it is the right thing to do, because he deserves it. There are certain reactions to a child's rejection of God that are appropriate, but shock is not really one of them. Job 5:7 says we are 'born to trouble as surely as sparks fly upwards.' We live in 'the woods between the worlds',[16] in the kingdom of God, but waiting for its full impact. Things go wrong; there is pain and suffering and tragedy and grief. We don't always get the happy ending we long for. It may sound impossible, but there is peace to be found in an acceptance of that reality, in an acknowledgement that when our children are not Jesus' followers it doesn't mean that we have failed as parents, and it doesn't mean that God isn't good. The first step to living this situation well, then, is accepting it. God doesn't shelter his people from trouble, but he does sustain us in it.

Harriet knows as well as anyone that Christians are not protected from suffering. She has two daughters, one from her first marriage, one from her second, and her second husband had three children. She and William, her second husband, became Christians early in their marriage. One of her stepsons committed suicide when he was 18, which worsened William's mental health issues, and he became harsh and unkind towards the girls. Gemma, Harriet's eldest daughter, became anorexic and began self-harming. Her

---

[16] A place in CS Lewis's Narnia book *The Magician's Nephew*

relationship with her stepfather was incredibly destructive and, as a result, she ceased to trust God. Harriet says, 'When

I realised God is there for me and for the girls

William was shouting at the girls, I remember crying and saying that my own father would never have spoken to me like that. God said to me,

"he may not be here, but I am". That was the turning point. I realised God is there for me and for the girls. Since then, I have learnt to take everything to him.'

Oops!

There is no way we can be perfect parents. Admitting the ways we have let down God and our children is humbling and painful, but there is grace. 1 John 1:9 says: 'If we confess our sins, he is faithful and just and will forgive us ...' All of us will have made mistakes. All of us will make more. But God freely offers us forgiveness, and we need to take it, and be the kind of people who offer it with the same generosity.

When our children become adults, they become responsible for their choices. And then what we need to focus on is ourselves. We need to handle ourselves within these relationships in a way that reflects God's character; as John White says, 'God calls us to be to our children what he is to us. Therefore, we are not to base our relationship with them on any supposed results of the relationship but on what is right. It follows that if God's greatest desires for his creatures have not always been fulfilled, our desires for our children may not always be fulfilled either …'[17] He continues to say that the question to ask about our approach as parents is not 'does it work?', but 'does it reflect God's mind?' God's mind towards us is faithful, loving, merciful, long-suffering – but never controlling.

Becca tells her story: "When we moved house and church when I was 11, I started to drift away from church and I was allowed to do this. I suppose on some level I still believed, but Mum and Dad longed for me to have a living faith, even if they didn't pressurise me about it.'

She continues, 'In my early twenties I was diagnosed with a significantly life-shortening medical condition. It shook what faith I had considerably, and led me to a place of uncontrollable rage and hurt, a place where I no longer recognised God. But even in my darkest hours, when I

So … my journey isn't over, and I am beginning to rebuild my faith

decided God was an empty platitude, I longed to belong. My parents had an honest, accepting, joyful approach to faith, and they set me up to be always seeking, always

---

[17] John White, *Parents in Pain,* IVP, 1979, p163,4

looking to encounter God. So my journey isn't over, and I am beginning to rebuild my faith.'

As for me, I will serve the Lord

Where do we go from here? We go towards the heart of God. We look to develop the mind of Christ, to love our children more and more as he does, to show them God's character through our own and through the way we conduct our lives and relationships. We say sorry when we mess up, and start again. We let go of any sense of control over their destiny. And we pray, as people have prayed across the ages, that our loved ones would have their eyes opened to the truth that has been revealed to us:

'I pray that out of his glorious riches he may strengthen you with power through his Spirit in your inner being, so that Christ may dwell in your hearts through faith. And I pray that you, being rooted and established in love, may have power, together with all

... to him who is able to do immeasurably more than all we ask or imagine

the Lord's holy people, to grasp how wide and long and high and deep is the love of Christ, and to know this love that surpasses knowledge – that you may be filled to the measure of all the fulness of God.

'Now to him who is able to do immeasurably more than

all we ask or imagine, according to his power that is at work within us, to him be glory in the church and in Christ Jesus throughout all generations, for ever and ever! Amen' (Ephesians 3:16–21).

Using **Keeping Faith** as a group resource

There are almost certainly other Christian parents you know – in your church, your friends – who will share some of the concerns raised in *Keeping Faith*.

If you'd like to talk with others about the issues raised in this book, you will find some discussion questions for each chapter at: www.scriptureunion.org.uk/keepingfaith.

Use the questions as conversation starters. If you know each other well enough you might also want to take time to pray for one another.

Further reading

Gavin Calver, *Disappointed with Jesus?*, Monarch, 2010

Nathan Foster, *Wisdom Chaser*, IVP, 2010

Andy Frost, *Losing Faith, Authentic Media*, 2010

Daniel Hahn, *Teaching Your Kids the Truth About Consequences*, Bethany House Publishers, 1995

Rob Parsons, *Bringing Home the Prodigals*, Hodder & Stoughton, 2003

Rob Parsons, *Getting Your Kids Through Church Without Them Ending Up Hating God*, Monarch, 2011

Rob Parsons, *The Sixty Minute Family*, Lion Hudson, 2010

Danny Silk, *Loving our Kids on Purpose*, Destiny Image Publishers, 2008

John White, *Parents in Pain,* IVP, 1979

Books by the same authors

Jo Swinney:

Through the Dark Woods, Monarch, 2006
Cheerful Madness, Monarch, 2008
God Hunting, Scripture Union, 2011

Katharine and Richard Hill:

Rules of Engagement, Lion, 2005

 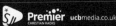

Grab a God moment

in your busy life...

It's so easy to get caught up in everyday life and forget to spend time reading the Bible. **WordLive** has been created to fit into your life and deliver God's Word to you where you are.

WordLive is an exciting online experience that puts the Bible at your fingertips.

WordLive's range of creative approaches helps you to meet God through the Bible and prayer: watch a video, listen to a podcast, dig deeper into further study or dip into creative prayer and meditation.

Thousands of people are already using **WordLive** to transform their experience of the Bible and deepen their relationship with God.

You can too!

Try WordLive today by visiting www.wordlive.org

Keeping Faith *is also about keeping a lot more – keeping hope, keeping going as well as keeping loving. The words of this book will be a sweet sound for many families in a near silent world where real doubts bring real struggles. Read and be encouraged to renew faith both in a God of love and in the ones we love.*

Alan Charter, Director, Children Matter!

This wonderful book faces up to the challenging issues involved head on while providing comfort and hope at the same time. Read this and realise that you haven't failed and are not alone.

Gavin Calver, National Director, Youth for Christ

Having spent many an hour in a car with Katharine as we tour speaking about being a mum, this book was exactly as I expected it to be: honest, thoughtful, encouraging, wise and full of faith in the midst of real life. Each of us who are Christian parents need a dose of reassurance as we navigate the journey of faith with our children. This book is an insightful, honest, positive and thought-provoking reminder of the power of unconditional love in our homes, and I know I will return to it time and time again for a little more encouragement along the way.

Cathy Madavan, freelance speaker, writer and communications consultant

In writing about this sensitive and important issue that affects so many families, Katharine and Jo exhibit understanding, wisdom and candour. Giving a clear way forward – while being careful not to overlook the needs of the children concerned – this book will be a lifeline for parents.

Rt Rev Mike Hill, Bishop of Bristol

Katharine and Jo write with insight and compassion. This book will provide hope, advice and encouragement to thousands of Christian parents whose children are going in the opposite direction to the one they had hoped or indeed prayed for.

Steve Clifford, General Director, Evangelical Alliance

Those of us with kids who have walked away from faith or who are close to doing so will thank God for Jo and Katharine's book. Their honesty, wisdom and compassion drip through every page as they inspire us with hope for the journey ahead. Read it and find accessible, practical help and a glimpse of the bigger picture.

Dr Krish Kandiah, Evangelical Alliance